Self, World, and Language: Robert Lowell's *Life Studies*

Self, World, and Language:
Robert Lowell's *Life Studies*

Date : 25 February 2010
Author : Hong-Pil Lee, Ph.D.
Publisher : Yeun Soo Kim
Published by Chonnam National University Press
77 Youngbong-ro Buk-gu, Gwangju, Korea 500-757
Registration : 21 May 1981 No. 53
ISBN : 978-89-7598-791-5 (93840)
Price : 13,000
http://altair.chonnam.ac.kr/~cnup

이 도서의 국립중앙도서관 출판시도서목록(CIP)은 e-CIP홈페이지(http://www.nl.go.kr/ecip)에서 이용하실 수 있습니다. (CIP제어번호: CIP2010000634)

Self, World, and Language: Robert Lowell's *Life Studies*

Hong-Pil Lee

Chonnam National University PRESS

In memory of my parents

Preface

One of my mentors in the United States, as he left for a college in Los Angeles, gave me a copy of John Ashbery's *A Wave* as a gift. On the inside cover he wrote a note saying that he hoped I would become "a passionate and eloquent teacher of poetry." About twenty years have passed since I completed my doctoral dissertation on Robert Lowell's *Life Studies*, but a question has haunted me for a long time: whether I have taught my students successfully and lived up to my mentor's wish. The answer is easy and I have come to the conclusion that I fell short of becoming "a passionate and eloquent teacher of poetry." My fifteen years of teaching have given me a strong sense that I need to better my earlier understanding of Robert Lowell. Teaching American poets, particularly whenever I have encountered Lowell, I found myself attracted to his way of "life studies," and this has brought me to reflect upon my own "life studies." One benefit from reading Lowell's *Life Studies* was that it helped me to take a deeper look at my own past. I believe that Lowell's "life studies" were very successful in that he could expand his self to the extent that he was able to reconstruct his relationship with the members of his family.

My understanding of Maurice Merleau-Ponty's phenomenology has helped me read Lowell's reconstruction and expansion of his own world. Although my original interpretation of Lowell's *Life Studies* through Merleau-Ponty's phenomenology was written some twenty years ago, this time span has not caused me to alter the initial combination or its interpretation; rather I find that it rings truer and truer as the years go by. This recognition has lessened my hesitation at publishing my dissertation and has led me to revise the chapters one by one.

This present volume adopts Maurice Merleau-Ponty's existential phenomenology and explores the self-investigation found in Robert Lowell's *Life Studies.* It particularly seeks to explore the ways in which the poet arrived at a sense of identity through engaging the external forces of life such as family, society and culture. Merleau-Ponty's *être-au-monde*, a modification of Husserl's intentionality, elaborates a theory of human communication which results from a complementary operation between the subject and the object. His thesis illustrates not only the possibility but the inevitability of the subject's coexistence with others and with the external world. Merleau-Ponty's phenomenology suggests a shared existence between the human subject and the world.

In *Life Studies,* Lowell places himself in the already-experienced world, i.e. the past. To position himself in the past is thus to re-experience and re-express his own self in language and to further question and seek out his identity in the world. I regard Lowell's *Life Studies* as the poet's personal perception of his past and as a journey toward an articulated discovery of his identity within the world of which Merleau-Ponty speaks. This book is a reading of *Life Studies* and focuses on the ways in which the poet examines the self by engaging himself with the external forces. These are the very forces, according to Merleau-Ponty, that the self must engage dialectically in order to come to a sense of its own subjectivity. The first chapter presents the theoretical background for a reading of *Life Studies.* In the second chapter, I examine the poet's declaration of his journey as "down-to-earth," which suggests his abandonment of his religion and reveals his view of human civilization. The third chapter deals with the fate of the poet's self by situating his family in the context of American history and culture. Chapter Four addresses the self which grows through interacting with the world. I present the poet's self in an ongoing dialogue with his family, especially treating the ways in which the poet comes to understand the world and forgives his parents and grandparents, with whom he once was strongly at odds. The fifth chapter seeks to explore how the poet's self aggrandized itself through a re-experience of his personal afflictions. The final chapter, concentrating on "Skunk Hour," examines how the poet created a reconciliation between the self and the tormenting world and how the poet's perception of the world led to the expression and establishment of the self in the world.

Table of Contents

Preface — v

Chapter 1. Introduction — 1

1. *Life Studies* and Contemporary American Literature — 1
2. Socio-Cultural Background of Mid-Century American Poetry — 10
3. Theoretical Preparation — 21

Chapter 2. From the "City of God" to the "City of Man" — 35

Chapter 3. The Self Incarcerated in the Family — 57

Chapter 4. The Self Remapped in the Family — 92

Chapter 5. Madness, Tranquilization, and the Self — 122

Chapter 6. "Skunk Hour": Completing *Life Studies* — 152

Bibliography — 162

Chapter 1

Introduction

1. *Life Studies* and Contemporary American Poetry

Robert Lowell's *Life Studies* opens with the poet "On the train from Rome to Paris," which implies Lowell's metaphorical journey to locate his self in the world. The opening poem "Beyond the Alps" outlines the direction of that poetic tour: the quest for his suffering self---"the blear-eyed ego." By putting his private situation into a broad historical and geographical context, Lowell seeks to investigate the perimeters of his life in self-revealed language. Put another way, Lowell explores his inner self by displaying his private experiences on to the external world. Lowell pushes his private past into these poems by unreservedly disclosing his family's shame and humiliation as well as his own madness and imprisonment. In this confrontation with the demons of his life, Lowell relies exclusively upon his own perceptions, without recourse to any transcendental reality or to the concept of an intangible deity. Most important, such a downright engagement with autobiographical data shows that the poet intends to put his whole life into question, thereby identifying his presence in the world.

Such overt self-expression---placing the self in the center of poetry, as M. L. Rosenthal has suggested---was like a reformation in the history of American poetry[1]. James E. Miller identifies "the two poles of American poetry" in Whitman and Eliot, and remarks that "the Eliot dominance" inaugurated by *The Waste Land* (1922) began to "wane by the late 1950s and continued to fade in the 1960s."[2] Indeed, Allen Ginsberg's *Howl and Other Poems*

---

1) Self-expression became a dominant poetic mode in mid-century American poetry. Discussing the tendency of self-expression in contemporary American poetry, M. L. Rosenthal captures three different aspects: "The Self seeks to discover itself through the energy of its insights into reality and through the sensuous excitement generated in it by its experience of reality"; ". . . our poetry of political and cultural criticism centers on the individual as the *victim"*; ". . . the private life of the poet himself, especially under stress of psychological crisis, becomes a major theme. . . . the idiom of our poetry can be at once private and public, lyrical and rhetorical." See M. L. Rosenthal, *The New Poets: American and British Poetry since World War II* (New York: Oxford UP, 1967) 13-15.

2) James E. Miller, Jr., *The American Quest for a Supreme Fiction: Whitman's Legacy in the Personal Epic* (Chicago: U of Chicago P, 1979) 10.

It should not be overlooked that even though addressing the autobiographical self becomes popular in the mid-twentieth century, the

(1956) offered American Poetry a new paradigm. In some sense, too, Robert Lowell's *Life Studies* (1959) hastened the end of the Pound-Eliot era in terms of its poetic themes and styles. The revolutionary experiment of the mid-century poetry was undeniably against "an orthodoxy" which "derived from the authority of T. S. Eliot and the new critics."[3] Although many mid-century American poets were schooled under the influence of modernist poetics, later, when they came into their own, some of them fashioned an anti-modernist mode of po-

---

poets in the fifties are not the first to engage themselves in their poems. As a matter of fact, there has been a strong tendency to express the self in American literary tradition since the nineteenth-century. In *The Cycle of American Literature*, Robert Spiller suggests the two directions of American poetry that were formulated in the nineteenth-century:

> By 1890 two roads of future development in American literature were clearly marked: the road that led to an open acceptance of nature and of things as they are, and the road that led inward to an explanation of the consciousness to tradition, to restraint, and to concern for form.

Spiller goes on to say that Whitman and Mark Twain took the first road, and Poe, Hawthorne, Henry James, Faulkner, Dickinson and T. S. Eliot the second. According to him, then, Whitman and Dickinson established the two main streams of American poetry; one direction reached its fruition in T. S. Eliot and Pound, and the other in Lowell, Berryman and Plath. Indeed, twentieth century American poetry, through a number of its experiments, has maintained its continuity with the nineteenth-century. Like a paradigm shift, American poetry has repeated continuity and discontinuity in terms of its direct expression of the poet's self. See Robert Spiller, *The Cycle of American Literature* (New York: Macmillan, 1955) 163.

3) Donald Hall, *Contemporary American Poetry* (Baltimore: Penguin Books, 1965) 17.

etics under which poems like *The Waste Land* or *Cantos* were inconceivable[4]. Allen Tate's comment on *Life Studies* (". . . it's not poetry"), for instance, draws a distinctive borderline between modernist poetry and the poetry since the 1950s.

What, then, was the modernism that contemporary American poets went against? To answer the question, it is necessary to take a brief look at the basic credo of the modernism which dominated literary movements in the first half of this century. Since the appearance of Eliot's essays "Tradition and the Individual Talent" (1917) and "Hamlet and His Problems" (1919), poetry as escape from personality became one primary element of the modernist poetic fashion. In "Tradition and the Individual Talent," Eliot sets out an "impersonal theory of poetry" which emphasizes the importance of personality and emotions in the poet and yet argues for an escape from personality as the key prerequisite for poetry. The artist's escape from personality is to be achieved through a process

---

4) Not every contemporary poet denied the modernist poetics. "Black Mountain poets" such as Robert Duncan, Charles Olson, and Robert Creeley are known as the followers of Pound. M. L. Rosenthal remarks: ". . . what Olson calls 'projective verse' is very far neither from Pound's periplum nor, for that matter (however it horrify the projectivists), from Eliots's 'objective correlative.' The terms are shifted, however, from attention to the sequence of images and other concrete effects to any form of externalization of the speaking psyche by way of the medium of language." See M. L. Rosenthal 145-46. And some critics find that like Pound, projectivists often employ images-collection, a montage of historical information, and an intellectual connection of images. For example, Charles Olson's epic *The Maximus Poems* is comparable with Pound's poems in many ways.

of transmutation. To explain how the poet's mind works in the act of creation, Eliot uses a chemical analogy: if oxygen and sulphur dioxide are combined with platinum, they produce sulphurous acid; yet the platinum itself remains intact and the new gas does not contain any traces of platinum. That is, the good poet, through an artistic process, ought to conceal one's personal voice or purely private impressions behind a poetic persona; likewise, the good critic must seek a certain objectivity by focusing on the work itself rather than on the poet. In his essay on *Hamlet*, Eliot speaks of the actual transformation of emotion:

> The only way of expressing emotion in the form of art is by finding an "objective correlative"; in other words, a set of objects, a situation, a chain of events which shall be the formula of that *particular* emotion; such that when the external facts, which must terminate in sensory experience, are given, the emotion is immediately evoked.[5] (original italics)

It is the objective correlative that alters personal emotion into "the form of art." Thus, elements that can be identified with the artist's biography get transmuted in the process of creation and emerge only as the personality of the work itself.

Similarly, Ezra Pound talks about the reductions of emotions in art in his formulation of the imagist project: "Emotion, seizing upon some external scene or action,

---

5) T. S. Eliot, *The Sacred Wood* (London: Methuen, 1964) 100.

carries it in fact to the mind; that vortex purges it of all save the essential dominant or dramatic qualities and it emerges like the external original."[6] For Pound, writing poetry is the process in which the poet, denying any kind of personal interpretation of the external object, creates a concrete language to represent the world through a linguistic technique. Take "In a Station of the Metro" for example; this poem purges all emotions from its denotative, succinct language. For modernist poets like Eliot and Pound, molding their personal experiences into objective language was the goal. The Eliot-Pound poetics firmly established the objectification of poetry in their reworking of personal experiences. Since they stressed impersonality and objectivity through a wide knowledge of classical literature and "high intelligence," poetry tended to be intellectual, allusive and highly indirect. They turned to classical mythology for literary experience and looked to French Symbolist poetry and Metaphysical poetry for their use of irony, wit, and conceit. As a result, what readers of their poetry needed was not biographical knowledge of the poets but a sophisticated knowledge of classical literature and the literary conventions of previous ages.

As Robert Bly observes, modernist poets had "more trust in the objective, outer world than in the inner world."[7] Indeed, they projected their emotion or inner

---

6) Ezra Pound, *Selected Prose 1909-1965,* ed. William Cookson (New York: New Directions, 1973) 345.

7) Robert Bly, *American Poetry: Wilderness and Domesticity* (New York: Harper & Row Publishers, 1990) 8.

vision into the outer world by using external objects or events---Eliot's "objective correlative." Although to a lesser degree than Pound and Eliot, William Carlos Williams and Wallace Stevens also avoided the direct involvement of their personal experience in their poems. Williams eradicates private experiences by projecting them into external objects, and Stevens fictionalizes himself in the working of the imagination. Consequently, there remains only a very small amount of the poet's autobiographical self in the poems.

Just as Pound and Eliot broke from Victorian modes of poetry in the early twentieth century, so poets in the 1950s fashioned a poetics that revolted against their predecessors. Their most conspicuous revolt consists in the direct treatment of their autobiographical facts and the explicit revelation of the self in their poetry. In *Cry of the Human*, Ralph J. Mills, Jr. observes the tendency toward self-creation in contemporary poetry:

> The contemporary poet re-creates himself as a personality, an identifiable self within his poetry, that is, of course, a self who has been selected and heightened in the process, captured in essence, and so is not perhaps a full likeness of the author as a physical, workday person outside the poem yet could not be mistaken for someone else. . . . [w]e recognize a certain maganimous gesture in their acts of creation, a profoundly touching and human gesture through which the poet voluntarily stands exposed as "creation's very self" before us.[8] (ellipsis mine)

---

8) Ralph J. Mills, Jr., *Cry of the Humans: Essays on Contemporary American*

Unlike poets in the 1920s who hid themselves behind language and tradition, many poets since the fifties, preferring personal experiences to tradition, have embraced autobiography as a major theme in their poetry. Instead of relying on classical literature, contemporary poets have sought to build a mythology out of their own experiences in the world. As Marjorie Perloff remarks, Lowell "creates a mythology out of his own life and those of his friends, relatives, or historical counterparts."[9] Similarly, John Berryman, Anne Sexton and Sylvia Plath come closest to M. L. Rosenthal's term "Confessional Poets" in that the poets themselves become the speakers in their poems, and their private experiences of madness, failure, and alienation become the subjects of their poetry.

As the mode of poetic themes altered, mid-century American poets adopted a technique different from the poets of the 1920s and 1930s. Unlike their predecessors, the poets in the 1950s tried to grasp the immediacy of daily experiences and transform them into art, a process that demanded a new creative apparatus. James E. B. Breslin, for example, elaborates on the radical change of theories and practices of poetic form the period saw:

> During this time, in fact, the Beats, the Confessional poets, the Black Mountain, New York, and Deep Image groups proposed a range of alternatives to the established mode, and they provided the leading sources of

---

Poetry (Urbana: U of Illinois P, 1975) 7-8.

9) Marjorie G. Perloff, *The Poetic Art of Robert Lowell* (Ithaca: Cornell UP, 1973) 36.

> the new paradigms for poetry that became visible in the late fifties and early sixties. These clusters of poets differed from each other in fundamental ways and in some instances were mutually antagonistic; but they agreed in **their renunciation of the well-made symbolist poem and in their search for poetic forms that could capture temporal immediacy, for the language of a breakthrough back into life.**[10] (emphasis mine)

The demands of self-revelation and promptness of personal experience in the new poetry could not be met by the conventional poetic forms which stressed, among other things, precise prosody of rhyme and meter. Mid-century American poets had therefore to reject the complex techniques of modernist poetry in favor of themes and techniques which accommodated the self and private experience. In the formulation of this revolutionary poetics, Lowell's *Life Studies* was an influential and pioneering text. *Life Studies*' prose and poetry, expressing a variety of modes with the self as the work's articulating center, was revolting less than revolutionary in the fifties and was hardly able to be written in the modernist poetics of Eliot, Pound, Tate and Ransom.

---

10) James E. B. Breslin, *From Modern to Contemporary American Poetry, 1945-1965* (Chicago: U of Chicago P, 1987) xv.

2. Socio-Cultural Background of Mid-Century American Poetry[11)]

Perhaps one of the best ways to gauge the cultural mood of post-World War Ⅱ America is through its literature. Although World War Ⅱ ended in victory, many in the country felt a sense of crisis that was reflected in contemporary poetry. M. L. Rosenthal elaborates "the new poetic scene":

> . . . since the war of 1939-45 the most striking poetry in the English language has taken on a new coloration, in effect a new sense of unease and disorder. Behind it is the feeling, perhaps, that the humanistic way, which traditionally educated and romantic modern men still propose to protect, and indeed to project into a Utopian future, has already been defeated and is now no more than a ghost. It is that feeling which Robert Lowell in one of his poems calls, self-ironically, 'our universal *Angst*'---a heart-heavy realization that remorseless brutality is a condition not only of the physical universe but also of man himself.[12)] (ellipsis mine)

It appears that the sense of crisis resulted from a variety of social, cultural, and political factors. Paul Breslin lists some of the disruptive elements present at the time:

---

11) In Part Ⅱ, I am much indebted to Paul Breslin's "Radical Poetics and Radical Politics," the first chapter of *The Psycho-Political Muse*, and to Ihab Hassan's "General Introduction," *Contemporary American Literature 1945-1972*. Some paragraphs are a partial summary from "Radical Poetics and Radical Politics."

12) M. L. Rosenthal 5.

"postwar social criticism, the subsequent onset of cold war, the New Left movement, and the revolt in the arts against reason and culture."[13] Nevertheless, many American intellectuals still envisioned the prospect of continuing economic prosperity. Although many of the industrialized countries after the second World War had severe economic problems, the United States enjoyed economic preeminence as well as military hegemony in the world. Obviously, the postwar economic superiority bred in many intellectuals an optimism that their country would continue to prosper and everyone could go into the middle class. This economic prosperity made some intellectuals believe that the country could dissolve any political conflicts. Daniel Bell's *The End of Ideology: On the Exhaustion of Political Ideas in the Fifties* (1960), for example, expressed that hope. As Ihab Hassan notes, however, optimism about economic progress was accompanied by insecurity about social progress:

> . . . the Marshall Plan begins to link and restore broken nations. The fervency of the late Forties, induced not only by the sense of justified victory, nor only by the rise of America into clear preeminence, expresses some hope in the possibilities of life at midcentury. But the Truman Doctrine soon certifies the realities of the Cold War; power politics begets caution, internal restraints. The reign of affluence cum conformity, broken sporadically by anti-Communist hysteria or Beatnik disaffiliation, follows in the Fifties during the Eisenhower years.

---

13) Paul Breslin, *The Psycho-Political Muse* (Chicago: U of Chicago P, 1987) 3.

> Secretary Dulles's notion of Massive Retaliation hangs in the air while the Silent Generation . . . founds its suburbias and its exurbias.[14)]

Besides, the economic prosperity was far from being equitably distributed, and the number of the poor went on to increase. Thus the political optimism also turned out to be an illusion. The social-political mood of the Cold War era which resulted from Senator Joseph McCarthy's harsh suppression of the ideological left merely helped turn social criticism from problems of class injustice to cultural malaise, from politics to the social psychology of contemporary life. Despite the vision of economic progress, the postwar American society engendered a sense of crisis among many intellectuals. As many intellectuals became aware of governmental interference in individual freedom, they saw the dark side of forced conformity and regarded the bureaucracy with suspicion. Numerous sociological publications which examined a new social setting and character emerged in this period. For example, John Galbraith's *The Affluent Society* (1958), C. Wright Mills's two books *White Collar* (1951) and *The Power Elite* (1956), and David Reisman's *The Lonely Crowd* (1950) and *Individualism Reconsidered* (1954) became bestsellers among the country's intellectual audience.

Generally speaking, America's intellectuals in the period distrusted the contemporary society reflected in public opinion because they felt that public opinion was too

---

14) Ihab Hassan, *Contemporary American Literaturre 1945-1972: An Introduction* (New York: Frederick Ungar Publishing Co, 1973) 3-4.

prone to governmental manipulation. Mills bitingly criticized the instrumentalization of rationality in social science as well as the uncritical acceptance of technological efficiency; he also castigated American universities for merely becoming centers for business and the military rather than research centers for the pursuit of knowledge. That is, the institutions of higher education in America were only concerned with imparting the skills that power groups demanded and producing only technicians, with the result that liberal education disappeared in American universities. In *The Lonely Crowd*, David Riesman, examining the changed social character and values in materialistic terms, calls the mode of conformity "other-direction." He explains:

> *What is common to all the other-directed people is that their contemporaries are the source of direction for the individual---either those known to him or those with whom he is indirectly acquainted, through friends and through the mass dedia. This source is of course "internalized" in the sense that dependence on it for guidance in life is implanted early. The goals toward which the other-directed person strives shift with that guidance: it is only the process of striving itself and the process of paying close attention to the signals from others that remain unaltered throughout life.*[15] (original emphasis)

The social trend Riesman draws on indicates that traditional values such as individualism, the Protestant work ethic, and inner direction disappeared, and the oth-

---

15) David Riesman and others, *The Lonely Crowd* (New Haven: Yale UP, 1950) 21.

er-direction had become the dominant mode of American character. The other-directed person, according to Seymour Martin Lipset, is characterized by "(1) orientation toward situational rather than internalized goals, (2) extreme sensitivity to the opinions of others, (3) excessive need for approval, (4) conformity on internal experience as well as on externals, (5) loss of achievement-orientation, and (6) loss of individualism."[16)]

A little later, in a similar vein, Herbert Marcuse, in *One-Dimensional Man* (1964), held that American democracy provides no more than nominal freedom; there exists an invisible exercise of social control with the subsequent tendency toward conformity; thus, individuals are dominated by huge external organizations and are unable to establish an individual dimension:

> Today this private space has been invaded and whittled down by technological reality. Mass production and mass distribution claim the entire individual, and industrial psychology has long since ceased to be confined to the factory. The manifold processes of introjection seem to be ossified in almost mechanical reactions. The result is, not adjustment but *mimesis*: an immediate identification of the individual with his society and, through it, with the society as a whole.[17)] (original emphasis)

---

16) Seymour M. Lipset, "A Changing American Character?," *Culture and Social Character,* eds. Seymour M. Lipset and Leo Lowenthal (New York: The Free Press of Glencoe, 1961) 140.

17) Herbert Marcuse, *One-Dimensional Man* (Boston: Beacon Press, 1964) 10.

As a result, Marcuse argues, there is no distinction between inner and external dimensions but only "one dimension." Similarly, R. D. Laing's *The Politics of Experience* (1967) examines the "other-directedness" in American society. He says that the others have been internalized to the extent that we call them ourselves: "Each person, not being himself either to himself or the other, just as the other is not himself to himself or to us, in being another for another neither recognizes in the other, nor the other in himself."[18)]

Alongside social, political, and cultural changes, some disciplines also underwent revisions in the late forties and the fifties. Discussing a characteristic of the late 50s American poetry, Paul Breslin locates the change of the poetic theme in "psycho-political" terms. The poets in the mid-1950s and the mid-1960s were concerned with liberation of their own consciousness:

> Although there was not a single dominant period style, several prominent group styles emerged at about the same time. Despite their differences, they share a concentration of poetry as engaged in the liberation of human consciousness from a false consciousness imposed by society. This notion of the poet's task can be traced back to Blake, Shelley, and Wordsworth. But the heritage of post-Freudian depth psychology, and its application to the question of how social authority is psychologically internalized, gives contemporary versions of the romantic aspiration a different emphasis and, to some

18) R. D. Laing, *The Politics of Experience* (New York: Ballantine Books, 1967) 74.

extent, a different content also.[19]

Indeed, Freudian psychology, a common store of diagnosis of individual and social problems, faced an alteration of its primary thesis in the 1950s, and the theories of revisionists were closely concerned with how individuals think and structure themselves amid social demands.

As for the conflict between individual desire and social demands, Freud is optimistic that it can be compromised within the mind, because the former ("pleasure principle") is dominated by the latter ("reality principle"). Focusing on rationality in human consciousness, he says that the demands of one's society are internalized into one's conscious self through the parents who also accepted them from their own previous adult adaptation; the ego, adjusting internal and external demands, handles the irrational demands of both id and superego, and further negotiates between these demands and the actual situation in the world. To cope with the conflicting claims in society, according to Freud, all one needs to do is to strengthen the conscious part of the ego, although the instinctive desires one has to repress continue to remain unchanged in the unconscious.

Since the late 1930s, a number of psychologists have attempted to revise the Freudian version of the ego. Denying what Freud defined as the human psyche, and emphasizing the interaction between the individual and

---

19) Paul Breslin xiiii.

culture, they redefined the human psyche with the help of cultural anthropology and concluded that human beings are culturally conditioned. Instead of the unconscious, they examined the way in which cultural aspects are internalized. That is, they concentrated on the conscious part of the human psyche which mediates between the self and the environment. For example, Harry Stack Sullivan, classifying six epochs of personality development, contended that each stage develops through interpersonal experiences like empathy, language acquisition, cooperation of compeers, group solidarity and competition. That is, cultural indoctrination is made through various kinds of contacts with the outside world from the early stage of childhood.[20)]

In *The Neurotic Personality of Our Time* (1937), Karen Horney proposed an unFreudian dynamic interaction between individual and culture. She complained: "Freud's disregard of cultural factors not only leads to false generalizations, but to a large extent blocks an understanding of the real forces which motivate our attitudes and actions."[21)] Opposed to Freud's definition of universal human nature, she maintained that culture is relative, and viewed neurosis only as a social manifestation in that if a symptom or mechanism is accepted behavior within a

---

20) For further discussion, see Harry Stack Sullivan, *The Fusion of Psychiatry and Social Science* (New York: W. W. Norton & Co., 1964) 198-226, and J. A. C. Brown, *Freud and the Post-Freudians* (London: Penguin Books, 1972) 163-73.

21) Karen Horney, *The Neurotic Personality of Our Time* (New York: Norton, 1937) 20-21.

culture, it might be considered to be normal within that culture:

> From resemblances between findings concerning our culture and those concerning other cultures we must not conclude that both are due to the same motivations. It is no longer valid to suppose that a new psychological finding reveals a universal trend inherent in human nature. The effect of all this is to confirm what some sociologists have repeatedly asserted: that there is no such thing as a normal psychology, which holds for all mankind.[22)]

Another theorist interested in the relationship between the individual and his society is Erich Fromm. He erects his theoretical foundation on two assumptions: first, "that the fundamental problem of psychology has nothing to do with the satisfaction or frustration of any instinct *per se*, but is rather that of the specific kind of relatedness of the individual towards his world"; and second, "that the relationship between man and society is constantly changing."[23)] According to Freud, individuals are innately equipped with a set of biological drives which society satisfies or frustrates. Although admitting these biological needs in human beings, however, Fromm argues that the way these needs are satisfied is "culturally or socially determined."[24)] That is, he makes a distinction between the biological needs in human beings and how those

---

22) Karen Horney 18-19.

23) J. A. C. Brown 150-51.

24) J. A. C. Brown 152.

needs are satisfied in the realm of culture. Against Freud's theory of the passive assimilation of culture, he emphasized the social process by saying that human nature is a cultural product created by human beings. He also acknowledges the volitional part of the self and the interaction between the individuals and society: ". . . the formation of individual character is determined by the impact of its life experinces, the individual ones and those which follow from the culture, on the temperament and physical constitution."[25] Fromm tries to express "not only how passions, desire, anxieties, change and develop as a result of the social process, but also how man's energies thus shaped into specific forms in their turn become *productive forces, moulding the social process*"[26] (original italics).

Unlike Freud, who claimed that the human ego (the rational part of mental faculty) is subject to cultural norms, the post-Freudians recognized cultural relativity, the interacting relationship between individuals and their society, and the volitional part of human instinct. That is, while Freud mainly emphasized the passive side of the human consciousness, they found its active side. Skeptical of the rational power of the mental faculty, post-Freudians underlined instinctual parts of the self; furthermore, some radical psycho-political theorists came to reverse the traditional reason-instinct hierarchy. For them, the power of instinct stood over against cultural sub-

---

25) Erich Fromm, *Man for Himself: An Inquiry into the Psychology of Ethics* (New York: Rinehart & Co., 1947) 61-62.

26) J. A. C. Brown 151.

jugation of adjustment.

The traces of such an intellectual movement may be uncovered in the highly subjective, self-investigative poetry which emerged in the fifties in opposition to objective and rational modernist poetry. Karl Malkoff points out such a tendency in contemporary American literature:

> In twentieth-century American poetry, the traditional boundaries of the self have come into question. Charles Olson, speaking for Objectivism, calls the ego a peculiar interposition between man and the rest of creation, thus challenging the outer boundaries. But there are inner boundaries as well. The unconscious, by definition, is separate from the conscious self, upon which it may nonetheless exercise some force. Inaccessible to voluntary investigation, the unconscious is often perceived as an alien power; it is understood to strike a crucial blow against the vestiges of free will, as if to be motivated by the unconscious were to be moved by someone or something other than ourselves. This interpenetration between conscious and unconscious assured at the least some questioning of the boundaries ascribed to them; and no modern poets have done more to erode these boundaries than the Confessionals.[27)]

Lowell and Plath prove Malkoff's point; their poems reflect the trend of the period Malkoff speaks of. Some mid-century poets recognized the culture norms which get imbedded in the individual's consciousness, and they attempted to free the self from the other-internalized

---

27) Karl Malkoff, *Escape from the Self* (New York: Columbia UP, 1977) 92.

consciousness. An investigation of the self became the common subject of postwar American poetry, a poetic trend for which Lowell undertook a pioneering job, followed by John Berryman, Anne Sexton and Sylvia Plath.

3. Theoretical Preparation

In many cases when the human subject (the self) is confronted with external forces like family, culture and society, the former takes on a political character because the latter tends to be repressive of individuals. When Alan Williamson labels Robert Lowell "a poet of politics," for example, he seems to suggest that the poet struggles to identify himself against these external forces. It is possible to argue that throughout *Life Studies*, Lowell engages in a political exercise particularly in terms of his sustained effort to seek his identity in the world. Yet in exploring his identity amid the external forces of life, Lowell chooses to have an ongoing dialogue with them. Rather than separate himself from the external world, Lowell chooses to remain within the world. Unlike Sylvia Plath who struggles to defeat a dark world through her own rituals, Lowell seeks a reconciliation between the repressive world and himself. Whereas Plath tries to transcend the private suffering the outer world imposes on her, Lowell exposes himself to the world by confronting his past. Inclined to accept the world, he refuses to polarize good and evil, love and hatred, right and wrong, annihilation and salvation; rather, he puts himself through the tormenting experiences of life such as shame, frustration and alienation. Such an active participation in the world not only leads him to understand the nature of human predicament but also helps him identify and define himself in the world. Most important, Lowell, through this intense participation in life, gradually gains a deep compassion toward his parents and his contemporaries. This is the process through which Lowell liberates himself from his disturbing past. Lowell's acceptance of and persistent dialogue with the world enables him to build a house of being in language, to use Martin Heidegger's term. In this respect, Lowell's journey into the world is both epistemological and ontological.

Life Studies is at once a perception of the poet's past and an expression of his identity toward the outer world. To use Maurice Merleau-Ponty's term, *Life Studies* is the poet's embodiment in the world which includes at once perception and expression. Particularly when grasped as a communication of the self and the lived world, and as an attempt to seek his identity within the world, Lowell's dialogue in *Life Studies* comes close to Merleau-Porty's central thesis: *être-au-monde.*[28)]

Before we take a look at Merleau-Porty's phenomenology, which I will use as a means to explore Lowell's

---

28) Merleau-Ponty's *être-au-monde* might look similar to Martin Heidegger's Being-in-the world. While Merleau-Ponty breaks the dichotomy of the subject-object relationship, Heidegger's *Dasein* places its primary stress on the constructive performance of the human subject in relation to the world. Unlike *être-au-monde*, *Dasein* is a mode of being, "an eternity which in each case I myself am." See Martin Heidegger, *Being and Time,* trans. John Macquarrie and Edward Robinson (New York: Harper & Row Publishers, 1962) 78.

practice of poetry, let us briefly examine the history of Western epistemology especially as it pertains to human perception. The problem of human perception has been one of the central issues in the history of Western philosophy. It was Descartes who stressed the primary role of the subject in perception, as his *Cogito* was based on the absolute certainty of the human consciousness. Later on, Kant, combining empiricism and rationalism, argued that we recognized the world in terms of our experiences. The two philosophers, according to Merleau-Porty, "made consciousness, my absolute certitude of my-self, appear as the condition without which there would be nothing at all, and they established the act of relating as the foundation of what was related."[29]

But empiricists like Locke, Hume and Berkeley stressed the passivity of the human mind, and they denied the human subject any constructive role. In varying degree, philosophers like Hegel and Marx contended that human beings are largely subject to their socio-cultual background. That is, they observed that human thinking is subject to externals such as history, culture and society. Under the influence of Hegel and Marx, Karl Mannheim locates a close relationship between the individual and society. In *Ideology and Utopia*, for example, Mannheim states that one cannot be independent of the socio-histrical background:

---

29) Maurice Merleau-Ponty, "What Is Phenomenology?," trans. John F. Banner. *Cross Current 6* (1956) 61.

> . . . it is more correct to insist that he [the individual] participates in thinking further what other men have thought before him. He finds himself in an inherited situation with patterns of thought which are appropriate to this situation and attempts to elaborate further the inherited modes of response or to substitute others for them in order to deal more adequately with the new challenges which have arisen out of the shifts and changes in his situation.[30] (ellipsis mine)

Not merely because a human being's past continues to dominate one's present mode of thinking and speech, but also because individual thinking and speech have their root in the culture and history of the society, Mannheim points out that individual action and use of language cannot be understood apart from a particular society.

On similar ground, the French structuralists, basing their views on the premise that the human subject is totally composed of the social culture one belongs to, considered individual speech or thought to be meaningful when combined with the underlying mode of human activities at a particular period. Ferdinand de Saussure, the pioneer of structuralist linguistics, suggested an innovative model of language which shows the relation between an individual sign and language system. The most conspicuous trait of his view of language is the denial of any relationship between a word and its referent. Philosophers like Locke, Russell, and Wittgenstein regarded words as

---

30) Karl Mannheim, *Ideology and Utopia,* trans. Louis Wirth and Edward Shils (New York: Harcourt Bruce Jovanovich, 1936) 3.

markers that convey notions of the world whose structures are derived through perception and later represented by language. However, Saussure observed that language is not a marker which simply refers to the things in the world, but a system of signs in which a signifier, the acoustical entity, and a signified, the concept, are united. According to him, these "two elements involved in the linguistic sign are both psychological and are connected in the brain by an associative link."[31] Thus, the relation between signifier and signified, he says, is "arbitrary."[32] In other words, there is no inherent connection between the concept and the sound except for cultual and historical convention. Therefore, it is not through some intrinsic connection between a sign and its referent, but through its difference from other signs in the system that each signifier creates its own meaning. That is to say, individual utterances of language have nothing to do with the individual speaker's creativity and are nothing but a combination of words which "always already" exist in the language system. Thus, Saussure argued that linguistic investigation of *langue*, the conventional rule of language, automatically leads us to a full understanding of *parole*, the individual performance of the language system. According to structuralists, there is no room for an individual speaker's creativity, and the human speaker is unable to avoid subjugation to the culture, the already-existing sign system.

Similarly, Jacques Lacan draws his basic premise that

---

31) Ferdinand de Saussure, *Courses in General Linguistic,* trans. Roy Harris (London: Duckworth, 1983) 66.

32) Ferdinand de Saussure 67.

the pre-determined Symbolic order dominates the human subject. He observes that Saussure's linguistic distinction between *langue* and *parole* corresponds to the Freudian relation between the unconscious and the conscious. Distinguishing "the Imaginary order" from "the Symbolic order" in the developmental stage of a child, Lacan elucidates the process in which the human subject moves to the state of subjugation. In the stage of the Imaginary order, Lacan explains, the child has no sense of separation between itself and the Other, and so is unaware of its own subjectivity. The mirror phase leads the child to formulate an *imago*, an ideal unified self ("specular I"), which is actually not ideal since the image is the result of the child's misrecognition of itself.

This mirror image changes when the father makes his appearance. The child undergoes prohibition against its libidinal relations with the mother---the first experience of the Oedipus relation. That is, the name of the father, identified as the figure of the law, initiates the child into the cultural norm. Confronted with the father's intervention, the child hides his desire for his mother in the unconscious. This experience of repression turns the child from "the specular I" to "the social I."[33] From the moment of entering into the Symbolic order, the child is subject to the grammatical rules which already exist in the culture into which the child was born. Particularly, the child functions by virtue of signifiers and cultural codes;

33) Jacques Lacan, *Écrits: A Selection,* trans. Alan Sheridan (New York: Norton, 1977) 5.

that is, the child becomes culturally dominated and constituted: "Man speaks . . . but it is because the symbol has made him man"[34)](ellipsis mine); "Symbols in fact envelop the life of man in a network so total that they determine "the shape of his destiny"[35)](ellipsis mine). According to Lacan, therefore, the child's acculturation which is manifest in language amounts to the loss of his/her subjectivity. That is, our internalization of social and cultural norms is inevitable. Whatever effort we make to resist the tyranny of culture is doomed to be subjugated by the use of language, the epitome of cultural practice.

By contrast, Edmund Husserl, founder of modern phenomenology, contended that human consciousness moves outward all the time. Convinced of the primacy of consciousness, he underscored the intentionality of human consciousness. Under Kant's and Husserl's influence, a number of existential philosophers such as Martin Heidegger and J. P. Sartre claimed that human beings themselves construct the meaning of the world. Maurice Merleau-Ponty, a revisionist of Husserl, however, turned his predecessor's primacy of consciousness into the primacy of perception. That is to say, by focusing on the human body and its relation to the world, he established a framework to examine the self and its intersubjectivity in culture and history.

Merleau-Ponty classifies traditional theories of percep-

---

34) Jacques Lacan 65.

35) Jacques Lacan 68.

tion into "pure exteriority" and "pure interiority,"[36] and remarks that empiricists such as Locke, Berkeley and Hume viewed perception itself as the primary source of knowledge. Centering on the passivity of the human consciousness, they considered perception to be a phenomenon in which an object is automatically reflected by consciousness or reflected upon in consciousness. On the contrary, intellectualists such as Descartes and Kant, emphasizing the human subject in the act of perception, turned to the activeness of consciousness in perception.[37] Merleau-Ponty, however, takes an eclectic stance toward the working of perception and sees perception as the result of interaction between world and consciousness.

His "primacy of perception" thesis argues that we are not only passive recipients, but also architects of the world:

> What, in fact, do we mean when we say that there is no world without a being in the world? Not indeed that the world is constituted by consciousness, but on the contrary that consciousness always finds itself already at work in the world. What is true, taking one thing with another, is that there is a nature, which is not that of the sciences, but that which perception presents to me, and that even the light of consciousness is, as Heidegger says, *lumen naturale*, given to itself.[38] (original italics)

---

36) Maurice Merleau-Ponty, *The Primacy of Perception,* trans. William Cobb (Evanston, IL: Northwestern UP, 1964) 4.

37) Merleau-Ponty calls philosophers like Kant and Descartes "intellectualists" in order to differentiate them from empiricists like Locke, Hume and Berkeley.

Our perception, according to Merleau-Ponty, is not simply dominated by the world itself because the perceived object is not what it was, but an object arranged by consciousness as a signified being. This thesis implies a constant dialectic interaction between the world as locus and consciousness as focus. At the very moment of the birth of knowledge, we are present in the world. Yet despite the indispensable contribution of perception to "our idea of truth," Merleau-Ponty says, we are not aware that perception precedes all models or conceptions of our knowledge: "We never cease living in the world of perception, but we go beyond it in critical thought---almost to the point of forgetting the contribution of perception to our idea of truth."[39] Thus, perception and the world's "thereness" together occupy the central place in Merleau-Ponty's phenomenological investigation of the origin of knowledge.

Most important, Merleau-Ponty's term *être-au-monde* provides the primary data not only for communication but also for our being in the world as well. When he says: "Man is before himself in the world and it is in the world that he knows himself,"[40] he implies that our being in the world itself connotes communicating with others as well as understanding the meaning of our being in the world. *Être-au-monde*, a modification of Husserl's intentionality which is the mode of the human conscious-

---

38) Maurice Merleau-Ponty, *Phenomenology of Perception,* trans. Colin Smith (London: Routledge & Kegan Paul, 1962) 432.

39) Maurice Merleau-Ponty, *The Primacy of Perception* 4.

40) Maurice Merleau-Ponty, "What Is Phenomenology?" 62.

ness constantly moving toward the objects outside the human consciousness, is engaged in all our relations to the world, others and self. Robert Detweiler explains:

> Intentionality itself is prompted and discovered by the knowledge that we are part of the world's thereness, and hence our intending of the world's constituents is possible only because we share the identity of those constituents. **To intend the object is thus to intend ourselves, and the phenomenological endeavor becomes a grand process of inseparable self-and-world recognition.**[41] (emphasis mine)

Thus, Merleau-Ponty's phenomenology becomes a human communication theory which is based upon man's embodiment in the world. In "The Child's Relations with Others," for example, he lays out his communication theory by elaborating on the process of a child's perception of himself/herself and others through the body.

While acknowledging that environment molds the child, Merleau-Ponty maintains that it is the child himself who organizes his surroundings. He refers to the child's "elasticity" in reacting to his environment, and his own response to what the surrounding poses. For instance, he illustrates the child's emotional relations with family members by explaining the effect that a newborn baby has on the child. With the coming of the new baby, the child learns his new identity in the family and how to cope with the new surrounding.

---

41) Robert Detweiler, *Story, Sign, and Self* (Philadelphia: Fortress, 1978) 9.

Merleau-Ponty gives us a dialectical account of the child's perception of his own body and of the other's body. He asserts that through the experiences of my own body I can interpret the other's body; also that through the other's body I can understand my own body. Merleau-Ponty says that there is a meeting point between my embodiment and the other's: "My consciousness is turned primarily toward the world"[42]; "The other's consciousness as well is chiefly a certain way of comporting himself toward the world."[43] Since the child cannot see his own body as a whole, he is able to understand his own through this understanding of the other's specular image. That is, awareness of my body is made with the reciprocal experience of my body and the other's body.

At the point of awareness of the distinction between my body and the other's, however, egocentrism emerges in the child. Nevertheless, the child is not separate from others; the child feels he is "in the other's body, just as he feels himself to be in his visual image."[44] Merleau-Ponty thus says that the "global identification of the child with his body" creates the "global identification of the child with others."[45]

While the advent of the mirror stage becomes the foundation for understanding the world and others, the child, at this point, becomes aware of the distinction between him and the world. After this stage, Merleau-Ponty

---

42) Maurice Merleau-Ponty, *The Primacy of Perception* 116.

43) Maurice Merleau-Ponty, *The Primacy of Perception* 117.

44) Maurice Merleau-Ponty, *The Primacy of Perception* 134.

45) Maurice Merleau-Ponty, *The Primacy of Perception* 135.

holds, the indistinction between me and the other does not take place as often as in the pre-mirror stage. However, he does allow that the indistinction comes in a different form in adult life, despite a great difference in its degree of sharedness. As man grows aware of the world and the other, he gains more perspectives in the world and thus becomes farther removed from communication which he had in his childhood. Nevertheless, communication continues even in adulthood because of our being in the world which implies constant interaction between the world and self.

As we have seen, Merleau-Ponty's thesis elaborates a theory of the human subject which results from a complementary operation between the subject and object rather than from a dichotomous division. The thesis illustrates not only the possibility but the inevitability of the subject's coexistence with others and with the external world. Richard C. McCleary rightly observes that the existential phenomenology of Merleau-Ponty embodies a social reality:

> I can perceive something objectively only if I can perceive it simultaneously from more than one perspective. Since I am actually embodied at each moment of my experience in a particular perspective, the basis for objectivity must be the simultaneous presence of others and their perspective in my field of presence. To be conscious is to constitute, and I could not posit another person as another myself without thereby constituting him as constituting in respect to the very act through which I constitute him. Only my body provides me with

> a way between the possible and the real. As my fundamental and original experience of a being which is inseparably both constituting and constituted, my body teaches me what I cannot learn in any other way.[46)]

In this respect, Merleau-Ponty's existential meaning is a shared meaning between the human subject and the world. As a field of experience, the world contains a variety of perspectives and each self constitutes its own point of view in it. The phenomenological "I" is a perspective in the world, yet each perspective is expressive of other possibilities. This tells us that the meaning of individual existence reaches its completion only when individual perspective is integrated with other perspectives.

In *Life Studies*, Lowell places himself in the already experienced world (the past); to position himself thus in the past is to reexperience and express anew his self in language, and, further, to question as well as seek his identity in the world. The opening poem, "Beyond the Alps," which describes Lowell's departure from Rome to Paris, is tantamount to his adoption of a new methodology with which to perceive the world. It signifies Lowell's desertion of Catholicism and transcendental reality and marks his descent from that world to the objective, outer world. The metaphorical journey to Paris, "our black classic," anticipates Lowell's archaeological quest for his past, a quest that ends with his arrival at the sence of his identity in the world in the final poem "Skunk Hour." I

46) Maurice Merleau-Ponty, "Translator's Introduction," *Signs,* trans. Richard C. McCleary (Evanston, IL: Northwestern UP, 1964) xviii.

regard *Life Studies* as the poet's personal perception of his past and as a journey toward an articulated discovery of his identity within the world that Merleau-Ponty speaks of. This study is a reading of *Life Studies* that focuses on the way in which the poet explores the self by engaging himself in the external forces such as family, society and culture. These are the very forces that, according to Merleau-Ponty, the self must engage dialectically in order to come to a sense of its own subjectivity.

In the next chapter, I examine the poet's declaration of his journey as down-to-earth, which suggests his abandonment of his religion and reveals his view of human civilization. The third chapter deals with the fate of the poet's self by situating his family in the context of American culture and history. Chapter four addresses the self that is growing by interacting with the world. I present the poet's self in an ongoing dialogue with his family, especially treating the ways in which the poet comes to understand the world and forgives his parents and grandparents with whom he once was at war. Chapter five seeks to show that the poet's self aggrandizes itself through a reexperience of his personal affliction. The final chapter, concentrating on "Skunk Hour," shows how the poet creates a reconciliation between the self and the tormenting world and how the poet's perception of the world leads to the expression and establishment of the self in the world.

Chapter 2

From the "City of God" toward the "City of Man"

The central framework of Robert Lowell's *Life Studies* is built upon a complicated interrelationship between the self and the world. The four poems in its first part not only draw the central structure of *Life Studies*, but outline a world in fragmentation as well. By doing so, the poet establishes a context from which he is able to undertake probing self-exploration. Of particular importance in this very context are the institutionalized customs, those powerful forces that have shaped human history and civilization. That is, the first part elaborates the topography of a fragmented external world which inhibits the poet's self but without which the self cannot attain a sense of identity. Violence, alienation, and madness, all of which abound in the three poems following "Beyond the Alps," attest to the disorienting forces in the world. The four poems in the first part of *Life Studies* herald a long, painful journey of the poet's own life studies in their relations with the poems in the following parts of the book.

The very opening poem in *Life Studies*, "Beyond the Alps," makes several points that are crucial to a meaningful reading of the entire volume. The poem declares itself as an itinerary for the poet's own life studies. The goal of the journey is neither toward any god, transcendental reality. In fact, Lowell consciously avoids such a reality and decides to center his creative energy in bodily perception and in the world, represented as the modern secular city which is still "breaking up."[1] To put it another way, he remains in the world, and thus such an acceptance of external reality lends itself to a consideration of Merleau-Ponty's phenomenology:

> Phenomenology is the study of essences; and according to it, all problems amount to finding definitions of essences: the essence of perception, or the essence of consciousness, for example. **But phenomenology is also a philosophy which puts essences back into existence, and does not expect to arrive at an understanding of man and the world from any starting point other than that of**

1) Robert Lowell, *Life Studies and For the Union Dead* (New York: Farrar, Straus and Giroux, 1964) 4. All subsequent citations from *Life Studies* are from this edition, hereafter referred to as *LS* with page numbers in parentheses.

> **'facticity.'** It is a transcendental philosophy which places in abeyance the assertions arising out of the natural attitude, the better to understand them; **but it is also a philosophy for which the world is always 'already there' before reflection begins---as an inalienable presence; and all its efforts are concentrated upon re-achieving a direct and primitive contact with the world, and endowing that contact with a philosophical status.**[2] (emphasis mine)

For Merleau-Ponty, the self is both constituted by and constitutive of its incessant interaction with the world. And such an interaction entails a dialogical relationship between the human subject and the world, precisely the kind of interaction which takes place in *Life Studies.*

Lowell's journey from Rome to Paris seems to imply that he will seek the self in the world and further that the poet-speaker intends to conduct an ongoing dialogue with the world. This poem announces a direction for the

2) Maurice Merleau-Ponty, "Preface," *Phenomenology of Perception,* trans. Colin Smith (London: Rouledge & Kegan Paul, 1986) vii. In a similar vein, Herbert Spiegelberg also uses quotations from Merleau-Ponty: "man is within the world (*au monde*); it is in the world that he recognizes himself." According to Merleau- Ponty, since we are "engaged" in the world, the quest for the self cannot be realized outside of its "incarnation" in it. To Husserl's maxim, "Turn into yourself: truth in the inner man," Merleau-Ponty respond: "Truth does not dwell only in the inner man, or rather, there is no such thing as an inner man." What the self finds is a "subject vowed (*voué*) to the world." The meaning of the English translation "vowed" here is close to "bound." In other words, the human subject grasps its meaning within the world. See Herbert Spiegelberg, *The Phenomenological Movement: A Historical Introduction* (The Hague: Martinus Nijhoff Publishers, 1984) 537-60.

entire book: that the poet will explore the self in the world. In this attempt to search for the self in external reality, he prefers descending to the earth rather than ascending to heaven. The determination to abandon the church constitutes an underlying commitment to examine the self unhampered by divine consideration. Only concerned with the self in the here and now, the poet centers on empirical experiences of reality in the world.

Lowell's physical move from Rome to Paris in "Beyond the Alps" mirrors a change in his inward paradigm. We no longer find "Lowell's deeply inward Catholicism, with its stress on universal guilt,"[3] as in *Land of Unlikeness* (1944) and *Lord Weary's Castle* (1946). In his early works, Lowell heavily employed Christian imagery. Many of the poems are embodiments of the Christian ideals left unfulfilled by America's founders. Rather than employing religious imagery as a medium of spiritual confession, Lowell directs it toward revealing the world's spiritual desolation. Herbert Leibowitz elaborates on Lowell's use of Christian imagery in his early poetry:

> The land of unlikeness of the title is partly America but mostly some country of the mind whose topography cannot be mapped with precision. It is only outwardly a Catholic duchy. True, the poems abound with references to Jesus' crucifixion, the Holy Ghost, and the Virgin Mary, anathema to the Puritans. True, the poet rails against the aridity of the Puritans. But, a Catholic con-

---

3) Alan Williamson, *Pity the Monsters: The Political Vision of Robert Lowell* (Westport, Connecticut: Greenwood Press, 1986) 17.

> vert descended from a distinguished New England family, he addresses Mary and Christ in the raw, driven idiom of Cotton Mather. Charon, the ferryman who figures so largely in the volume's imagery, is a Puritan helmsman, his raft a Mayflower, and Lowell, his passenger, a wandering soul ferried across the gulf of doubt and unknowing to a New Land that might or might not be hell.[4)]

Lowell adopts Christian imagery only to show the incompatibility between pious religiosity and the commercial pursuit and prosperity in the New World. As a result, most of Lowell's poems which use Christian imagery mock the Puritan dream. Using the frame of Christian doctrine, for instance, "Children of Light" castigates the spiritual decline and the subsequent rise of destructive energy (war). Most important, Lowell frequently employs Christian imagery to convey an apocalyptic vision of the world. For instance, "The Quaker Graveyard in Nantucket," which is "a hybrid of literary antecedents Catholic and Protestant,"[5)] embodies Lowell's dark vision of the world's fate.

Leibowitz has remarked that even though religion figures prominently in Lowell's early poetry, his poetic imagination is "empirical, concrete, not transcendental."[6)] In other words, even in the religious phase of his career

---

4) Herbert Leibowitz, "Robert Lowell: Ancestral Voices." *Salmagunda* 1 (1966) 26.

5) Philip Cooper, *The Autobiographical Myth of Robert Lowell* (Chapel Hill: U of North Carolina P, 1970) 23.

6) Herbert Leibowitz 30.

Lowell did separate the spiritual from the concrete. This tendency paves the way for the announcement of the "down-to-earth" in "Beyond the Alps." Indeed, Lowell descends to "the earth," trusting in his observations of the world rather than in institutional Catholicism. That is, bodily experience replaces apocalyptic vision in Lowell's poetry. Lowell's inward Catholicism changes to an outward expression: a bold, frank confession of his humiliating past. "Beyond the Alps" is the first poem that reveals the primary concern of the volume: a religious self-examination which exposes the extent to which institutional and external forces have shaped him. It observes and reflects on Christianity and civilization in a historical perspective.

The outer experience of reading a book on a train journey from Rome to Paris evokes inner experience: physically, the poet moves from Rome to Paris, from past to present, from the origin of civilization to its corrupt site in modern times, and from "the City of God" to the godless modern city:

> Life changed to landscape. Much against my will
> I left the City of God where it belongs.
> There the skirt-mad Mussolini unfurled
> the eagle of Caesar. He was one of us
> only, pure prose. I envy the conspicuous
> waste of our grandparents on their grand tours---
> long-haired Victorian sages accepted the universe,
> while breezing on their trust funds through the world. (*LS* 3)

Alan Williamson has characterized this departure from

the "City of God" as an "important turning point in Lowell's own career"[7]; James E. B. Breslin also sees it as "a metaphorical journey from a traditional and mythical order to a secular empirical one, the cruel and chaotic world of 'pure prose.'"[8] This amounts to Lowell's rejection of Christianity, "the City of God," which is also the birth place of modern civilization, including the culture of violence. Ceasar's predatory emblem (the eagle), handed down to Mussolini in modern Italy, raised violence and destruction around the world. Caesar's and Mussolini's destructive energy survives in every one of us: "He was one of us/ only, pure prose." As Stephen Yenser has pointed out, "the disintegration of Western culture in the areas of politics and religion" is the principal theme of the poem.[9] Lowell is convinced that Catholicism cannot be a stabilizing center for the fast disintegrating world around, and so longingly looks back on the days of the nineteenth-century optimism during which people found meaning in a mundane understanding of the world.[10] He

---

7) Alan Williamson 95.

8) James E. B. Breslin, *From Modern to Contemporary American Poetry, 1945-1965* (Chicago: U of Chicago P, 1987) 125.

9) Stephen Yenser, *Circle to Circle: The Poetry of Robert Lowell* (Berkeley: U of California P, 1975) 123-24.

10) As a protest against his ancestors, Lowell converted to Catholicism, in which he became dissatisfied once again. Irvin Ehrenpreis explains: "He[Lowell] was also converted to Roman Catholicism, the church peculiarly associated in Boston with the large population descended from humble Irish immigrants, natural enemies, in politics and culture, of his own class. But the poet already felt committed to a kind of moral vitality that could for only a limited time be expressed in Roman terms. During the period when his new-found church was something

envies the "grand tour" and the "long-haired Victorian sages" who "accepted the universe." Though for the most part secular and, in a sense, ridiculous, the Victorians were much happier than their descendents because they adjusted themselves to the outside world.

In Lowell's mind, the strength of nineteenth-century secularism becomes all the more obvious in the face of the dogmatism of modern Catholicism, reflected in the Vatican's declaration of the Virgin Mary's assumption into heaven:

> When the Vatican made Mary's Assumption dogma,
> the crowds at San Pietro screamed *Papa.*
> The Holy Father dropped his shaving glass,
> and listened. His electric razor purred,
> his pet canary chirped on his left hand.
> The lights of science couldn't hold a candle
> to Mary risen---at one miraculous stroke,
> angel-wing'd, gorgeous as a jungle bird!
> But who believed this? Who could understand?
> Pilgrims still kissed Saint Peter's brazen sandal.
> The Duce's lynched, bare, booted skull still spoke. (*LS* 4)

Christianity converted religious sanctity into bureaucratic

---

defiant of the Boston he had repudiated, and so long as the language, symbols, and ritual represented materials to be conquered and employed for explosive purposes, he could use Catholicism as an ingredient of poetry. But when it was only the faith he had to accept, the church came to seem as oppressive and self-contradictory as the code of his native class." Irvin Ehrenpreis, "The Age of Lowell," *Robert Lowell: A Collections of Critical Essays*, ed. Thomas Parkinson (Englewood Cliffs, N.J.: Prentice-Hall, 1968) 76.

authority; it merely gives rise to blind, collective obedience among its followers. The authority, which the Pope exercises, seems to make him a political, rather than a religious leader. Lowell's association of the Pope with such comical, modern elements as a purring "electric razor" and a "chirping pet canary" not only downgrades the papacy but exhibits Lowell's view of Catholicism as well. The combined image of an "electric razor" and a pet bird, purring-chirping on the Pope's left hand, is a travesty of the image of Christ sitting on the right hand of the Father. The element of mockery serves to reinforce his sense of disappointment with the church. And less powerful is the image of modern science, unable to probe and expose the falsity of the religious dogma. The above passage shows Lowell's loss of faith in the established church as well as his skeptical attitude toward modern civilization. Once again, Lowell underscores that Mussolini, an incarnation of violence, was born into the very city of God, and still remains there: "The Duce's lynched, bare, booted skull still spoke."

Lowell has now crossed the Alps, the "Romantic symbol of grandeur and spiritual elevation,"[11] and come down to the "earth." To come to the earth is to find the suffering self: "the blear-eyed ego kicking in my berth/ lay still." This picture of the poet as the prisoner of the existing human condition foreshadows the tormented self of the poet throughout *Life Studies*.

---

11) Marjorie G. Perloff, *The Poetic Art of Robert Lowell* (Ithaca: Cornell UP, 1973) 5.

Although critical of the classical civilization, the poet still longs for it:

> There were no tickets for that altitude
> once held by Hellas, when the Goddess stood,
> prince, pope, philosopher and golden bough,
> pure mind and murder at the scything prow---
> Minerva, the miscarriage of the brain. (*LS* 4)

But once Lowell recalls what the ancient civilization is, his nostalgia disappears. For the ancient civilization of Greece and Rome bore the seed of the disintegration which came to fruition in modern civilization. Politics, religion, and philosophy were once unified and represented by the Goddess. Yet the fact that Minerva, symbol of wisdom, is only "the miscarriage of the brain" exhibits fragmentation in civilization at that very moment of its birth.

Lowell rejects the idealized notion of civilization; instead, he accepts disintegration as a fact of civilization. Seen in the light of Lowell's condemnation both of the church and of civilization, it is clear that the departure from "the City of God" to "our black classic" and the descent from "that altitude" of the classical world to the earth is a starting point for an examination of the world. The departure shows Lowell's determination to seek out himself in the midst of the hopelessly fragmented world:

> Now Paris, our black classic, breaking up
> like killer kings on an Etruscan cup. (*LS* 4)

Lowell's entrance into Paris, "our black classic," is the beginning of the poet's journey in self-discovery. In this respect, the picture of the poet that emerges in the closing couplet is that of a man bent on pursuing his goal, not, as Breslin has remarked, "a helpless spectator of the chaos enveloping him."[12)]

While "Beyond the Alps" outlines the nature of civilization and discloses the itinerary of the poet's own life studies, the three poems following it present specific manifestations of the possible fragmentation Lowell finds in civilization, past and present, and further foreshadow the aspects of disintegration in Lowell's family that produced the anguished situations in his life. That is to say, the three poems epitomize the inhabitants and their world outside the "City of God" from which Lowell declares his departure in the opening poem.

"The Banker's Daughter," according to Stephen Yenser, presents "the theme of disintegration" which "is transposed to the level of family."[13)] "The Banker's Daughter," dealing with the division within the royal family of Renaissance France, shows disintegration in both the external version that is the state and in the individual family unit. The breakdown of the marriage of Marie de Medici and Henry IV is deeply entangled with religious and political complications; the queen's exile is also interwoven with the political chaos following the death of Henry IV. Lowell's account of the situation of the exiled

---

12) James E. B. Breslin 126.

13) Stephen Yenser 127.

queen before her monologue provides a vignette of the political culture in Renaissance France: political disorder and individual alienation.

The marital life of the king and the queen is in crisis:

> O cozy scuffles, soft obscenities,
> wardrobes that dragged the exchequer to its knees,
> cables of pearl and crazy lutes strung tight---
> O tension, groin and backbone! Every night
> I kicked the pillows and embroidered lies
> to rob my husband's purse. I said his eyes
> flew kiting to my dormer from the blue.
> I was a sparrow. He was fifty-two. (*LS* 5)

The king and the queen lead loveless lives. Above all, their telling age gap makes their marriage appear mismatched. What maintains their marriage is a combination of sex and money: "O tension, groin and backbone! Every night/ I kicked the pillows and embroidered lies/ to rob my husband's purse." The moral corruption is accompanied by tension and disorder in the family as well as in the country: King Henry's assassination and his son's expulsion of Marie de Medici for his political ambition.

King Henry, whose rule was marked by intense religious dispute between Protestants and Catholics, also witnessed the Bourbon-Hapsburg enmity, the political turmoil between the two royal families: "Your great nerve gone, Sire, sleep without a care./ No Hapsburg galleon coast off Finisterre/ with bars of bullion now to subsidize/ the pilfering, pillaging democracies,/ the pin-head priest, the nihilist grandee." Henry IV was assassinated by a fanatical Roman Catholic, Francois Ravaillac, who believed that God had chosen him to kill the Huguenot king and save the fate of Catholicism and papacy in France: "Murder cut him short---/ a kitchen-knife honed on a carriage-wheel."

Lowell describes the political disturbance in France which the sudden death of Henry IV created:

> Now seasons cycle to the laughing ring
> of scything children; king must follow king
> and walk the plank to his immortal leap.
> Ring, ring, tired bells, the King of France is dead;
> who'll give the lover of the land a bed?
> My son is adding inches in his sleep.
> I see his dimpled fingers clutch Versailles.
> Sing lullaby, my son, sing lullaby.
> I rock my nightmare son, and hear him cry
> for ball and sceptre; he asks the queen to die. . . . (*LS* 6)

The violence, including the death of the King of France which left the country in religious and political disorder, was handed down to the next generation. The widow, Marie de Medici, held the regency and protected the Jesuits, abandoning Henry's plan of war against the Hapsburgs. But Louis XIII, the heir of Henry IV, the most ruthless king in the history of France, banished his mother who opposed the king's orders to assassinate his minister: "she was exiled by her son and lived in a house lent to her by Rubens." The lesson from French history illustrates a relationship between individual tragedy and political organization. That is, Lowell coalesces public and private lives by linking "breaking up" of "killer kings" with the breakup of a family: the failure of Marie de Medici and Henry IV, the king's assassination, the religious and political turmoil of the country, and the exile of Marie de Medici by her son. This disintegration of the royal marriage, as Yenser notes, foreshadows "Charlotte Lowell's nagging and Commander Lowell's escape into the solitude of 'the Maritime Museum' and his midnight 'speculations,' as well as the situation referred to in 'To Speak of Woe That is in Marriage,'" all of which comprise a major theme of *Life Studies*.[14]

"Inauguration Day: January 1953" is a personal response to the American society which, according to the poet, has crumbled in the 1950s. When Karl Malkoff says of the poem that ". . . public world becomes part of Lowell's *private* experience,"[15] he suggests that much of the private dimension cannot be thought apart from public experiences. For example, the fact that the socio-political climate of the poet's time affects his feeling attests to the interrelationship between the self and the world.

Lowell's sketch of the 1950s, though based on his personal perception of the socio-political climate, goes beyond the personal. It expresses political sentiments during the country's McCarthyite period which other people might have shared. Politically paralyzed, the era is described as cold:

---

14) Stephen Yenser 127.

15) Karl Malkoff, *Escape from the Self* (New York: Columbia UP, 1977) 105.

The snow had buried Stuyvesant.
The subways drummed the vaults. I heard
the El's green girders charge on Third,
Manhattan's truss of adamant,
that groaned in ermine, slummed on want. . . .
Cyclonic zero of the word,
God of our armies, who interred
Cold Harbor's blue immortals, Grant!
Horseman, your sword is in the Groove! (*LS* 7)

The snow burying Stuyvesant creates a sense of silence and coldness. This feeling, along with the martial imagery that dominates the poem, epitomizes Lowell's satiric attitude toward the social and political morale of his time. The words "buried," "drummed," "charge," "armies," "Horseman," and "sword" all suggest violence associated with warfare. Particularly, the sound of "the El's green girders charge on Third" warns of an imminent militant assault. On a different level, they disclose apprehension which the government of a president who was once a military leader might cause. Such apprehension is underlined by Lowell's insertion of "warrior-administrators like Stuyvesant and Grant" who are all "impotent in spite of the military power that they command."16) The extremity of the cold season ("Cyclonic zero of the word") serves to sum up the present political paralysis: the totalitarian atmosphere which the governmental persecution of individuals engendered in the period.17)

16) Stephen Yenser 128.

17) Similarly, Albert Cook suggests the effectiveness of the poetic form to Lowell's theme: "The severity of the statement is enhanced by the

Such a configuration of the nation's past and present results in the cold vignette of the Eisenhower government:

> Ice, ice. Our wheels no longer move.
> Look, the fixed stars, all just alike
> as lack-land atoms, split apart,
> and the Republic summons Ike,
> the mausoleum in her heart. (*LS* 7)

Lowell here paints, in bitter words, a nation immobilized by a universal chill, a uniform state of the frozen that keeps the earth, the stars and everything in them separate, dead---"split apart." The image of the stars, all fixed in the sky like the wheels of modern civilization stuck in ice, conveys the country's deplorable condition as well as the poet's urgent desperation as the new government takes over: ". . . the Republic summons Ike,/ the mausoleum in her heart." The tight form of this poem serves, also, to mirror the poet's inner state of taut emotions as he contemplates the political landscape of the period.

The last poem of the first part, "A Mad Negro Soldier Confined at Munich," is a sketch of an isolated person, a victim of World War II. After investigating a disordered family and a disordered nation in the preceding two poems, Lowell displays the manifestations of this world in

---

tightness of the form, a sonnet unbroken between octave and sestet. The blunt stabs of the short, regular tetrameter lines gain added emphasis from the rhymes." See Albert Cook, *Prisms: Studies in Modern Literature* (Bloomington: Indiana UP, 1967) 54.

individual lives. And through the compressed picture of a disoriented individual, Lowell sets forth the madness which he finds in civilization. But before discussing "A Mad Negro Soldier," let us consider the way madness is associated with civilization in Lowell's poetry. In *Pity the Monsters*, Alan Williamson finds a similarity between Freud and the later Lowell in terms of their understanding of civilization:

> Lowell's questioning of civilization most closely resembles that of Freud in *Civilization and Its Discontents*, and that of the later, radical Freudians, Herbert Marcuse and Norman O. Brown. Like Freud, Lowell is concerned with the cost of civilization to instinctual satisfaction and even instinctual awareness; with the nature of the almost universal human sense of discontent and incompleteness, the possibilities and the illusions of a remedy. He is obsessed with outbursts of aggression and brutality, with their relation to civilized structures and/or to man's fundamental, biologically evolved nature.[18)]

Indeed, Freud, in a number of his writings, points out that the repression and deflection of the instinctive impulse, "sublimation," gives birth to civilization; according to him, there is an inverse relationship between the fulfillment of one's biological drives and the level of cultural achievement: ". . . the more suppression the more elaborate the culture and the greater the incidence of neurosis, and the less suppression the less neurosis but also the

---

18) Alan Williamson 2-3.

less civilization. Neurotics in fact are those who have fallen by the wayside in the drive toward a civilized society."[19] This paradoxical conflict between the pleasure-principle and the reality-principle (later as between Eros and Thanatos) constitutes the repressive forces of civilization which results in neurosis. In *The Ego and the Id*, Freud speaks of the destructive impulse in sublimation which the building of civilization demands: "After sublimation the erotic component no longer has the power to bind the whole of the destructive elements that were previously combined with it, and these are released in the form of inclination to aggression and destruction."[20] In constructing civilization, then, human beings are doomed to neurosis, aggression and destruction because without blocking their bodily needs, civilization cannot come into being. As his characterization of Minerva as "the miscarriage of the brains" suggests, Lowell's view of civilization is similar to that of Freud, and neurosis as a manifested form of civilized society appears in some poems of *Life Studies*. "A Mad Negro Soldier" prefigures this very theme.

The mental hospital in which the mad Negro soldier is imprisoned miniaturizes Lowell's inner vision of the outer world which is "full of sound and fury" signifying madness, alienation, violence and sex. The opening stanzas present a tormenting condition of the black American

---

19) J. A. C. Brown 19-20.

20) Sigmund Freud, *The Ego and the Id* (London: Hogarth Press, 1950) 80. For further discussion, see Sigmund Freud, *Civilization and Its Discontents*, trans. James Strachey (New York: Norton, 1961) 33-45 and Herbert Marcuse, *Eros and Civilization* (Boston: Beacon Press, 1966) 78-105.

soldier; that is, his confinement in a German mental hospital, his color, the brutal treatment from black American inmates, his possible language difficulty all combine to accentuate the soldier's alienation as an aspect of disintegration in the modern world. Indeed, totally estranged from the sane world, the soldier dwindles into a wild, sexually aggressive animal.

Institutionalized, the soldier responds to his surroundings in perversely instinctual ways; he becomes absolutely simplified and lives only for indiscriminate sex:

> Her German language made my arteries harden---
> I've no annuity from the pay we blew.
> I chartered an aluminum canoe,
> I had her six times in the English Garden. (*LS* 8)

The soldier's inability to communicate with other people, including his *Fraulein*, leads to further deterioration of the soldier's mental state. This miniaturized world continues to degenerate to such an extent that the archetypal garden here loses its traditional image and becomes a place like T. S. Eliot's waste land, characterized by barrenness and corrupt sex without generation. Most important, the insanity of the war and the madness of the soldier reflect each other, even as the soldier's inner and outer worlds collapse.[21)]

---

21) Philip Cooper contrasts the soldier's world and the outer world: "Mechanical clock, hierarchical lieutenants, aluminum canoe, formal English Garden, air-conditioned bowl. . . sketch the sterility of law and order against which the mad Negro's rich life moves" (ellipsis mine). See Philip Cooper, *The Autobiographical Myth of Robert Lowell* (Chapel

Lowell draws on the protagonist's helplessness before the large external force of war. War, a human artifact, has proved to be the product of man's loss of humanity and the willful promotion of brutality in the soldier. For instance, almost "lobotomized" like Lepke in "Memories of West Street and Lepke" in the fourth part of *Life Studies*, the mad soldier becomes fish, "fancy minnows" in the "air-conditioned bowl," and thus represents an individual overwhelmed by a huge external force:

> "Oh mama, mama, like a trolley-pole
> sparking at contact, her electric shock---
> the power-house! . . . The doctor calls our roll---
> no knives, no forks. We file before the clock.
>
> and fancy minnows, slaves of habit, shoot
> like starlight through their air-conditioned bowl.
> It's time for feeding. Each subnormal boot-
> black heart is pulsing to its ant-egg dole." (*LS* 8)

Electric shock therapy in the hospital and his memory of sex with his *Fraulein* are commingled together: "'Oh mama, mama, like a trolley-pole/ sparking at contact, her electric shock---.'" He has now become a slave of habit. This mad Negro soldier's world is our own world; his and ours form a composite world, the world Lowell calls "our black classic" in the opening poem. Furthermore, the mad Negro soldier's incarnation prefigures the victi-

---

Hill: U of North Carolina P, 1970) 64. Yet it seems to me that the mad soldier's world is an incarnation of the world where he lives.

mized self of the poet-speaker in the succeeding poems of *Life Studies.*

Life Studies as a collection of poems presents an almost complete structure for readers. Although the book was collected with the poems which were published in different periods, it creates a well-woven structure like a well-wrought prose. The first part I have talked about plays a role in heralding the succeeding parts which deal with civilization and culture as well as his own family members, non-biological family members and himself, all of whom are suffering under madness of civilization and culture. The characters in Part I of *Life Studies*, according to Steven Gould Axelrod, represent the exiles, the madmen, and the prisoners who will abound in the book. To some degree, they stand for Lowell himself.[22] Later poems name the actual figures who suffer under various pressures of the world, such as Ford Madox Ford, George Santayana, and Delmore Schwartz in the third part; moreover, Lowell himself is institutionalized in "Waking in the Blue" and "Memories of West Street and Lepke" in the fourth part of *Life Studies.* All these as well as the poet's father could all be characterized as alienated, even incarcerated inhabitants of the modern world. Lowell's portrayal of these figures in the first chapter is a testament to his keen awareness of Western civilization and his painful position in it, an awareness which will provide a context for the poet to investigate himself as

22) Steven Gould Axelrod, *Robert Lowell: Life and Art* (New Jersey: Princeton UP, 1978) 103.

one under threat from a hostile culture. Thus, entraining from the "City of God," and leaving behind the religious dependence upon transcendental reality, he has decided to seek himself and his fellow inhabitants in the "City of Man" who will appear in the succeeding parts of *Life Studies.*

Chapter **3**

The Self Incarcerated in the Family

The prose autobiography in Part Ⅱ of *Life Studies* focuses on the young Lowell's self shattered by the circumstances of his family. In the prose, Lowell quests for the origin of his own alienation to understand his present, by situating himself in the context of the whole spectrum of external forces like family, society, and culture, all of which, Lowell believes, interpenetrate and affect individual lives.

The exploration of the self within the past of his family makes up more than half of *Life Studies*; that is, Lowell's family becomes the central locus of his self-investigation. According to Lowell, what occurred in his family during his childhood vividly lives in him and becomes the basis of his adult life: "the vast number of remembered *things* remains rocklike," after "all the distortions of fantasy, all the blank befogging of forgetfulness" (*LS* 12-13, original italics). Thus a study of his family's past will lead to an understanding of his present. Lowell understands that in order to examine himself thoroughly, he must confront his family's tainted areas---shame and frustrations. In the process, as M. L. Rosenthal has remarked, Lowell willingly re-places himself in "a degraded or humiliating light."[1] The prose biography represents Lowell's full exposure to, rather than escape from, his past. Deliberately adopting prose form, Lowell attempts a dialogue with his past.

Since the present does not exist without the past, a dialogue with the past is an indispensible step to understanding our present. To engage ourselves in the "lived world" is to understand our present through a dialogue between the self and the experiences within the outer world. Merleau-Ponty claims: "To remember is not to bring into the focus of consciousness a self-subsistent picture of the past; it is to thrust deeply into horizon of the past and take apart step by step the interlocked perspectives until the experiences which it epitomizes are as if relived in their temporal setting."[2] As a dimension of our temporality in the world, according to him, the past

1) M. L. Rosenthal 36.

2) Maurice Merleau-Ponty, *Phenomenology of Perception* 22.

constitutes our present. To seek a precise location and meaning of the self, thus, it is necessary to examine the past. "91 Revere Street" is a study of Lowell's identity through an archaeological investigation of himself.

"91 Revere Street" is the only prose life study in *Life Studies*. It seems to me that Lowell's choice of prose is of a great significance. Prose, he was convinced, is a powerful medium for self-examination; he was also aware that choosing prose was an aberration from modernist poetics. When Ezra Pound and T. S. Eliot emphasized the prosaic quality in poetry, they had in mind a proselike clarity in poetry. Indeed, they were interested in prose only as a vehicle of poetic tenor. By adopting prose, however, Lowell seems to have a different effect in mind. The prose style in "91 Revere Street" serves as a medium for "unmerciful self-scrutiny."

Lowell frequently expressed his preference for prose, for instance, in his essay on the composition of "Skunk Hour":

> I had been giving readings on the West Coast, often reading six days a week and sometime twice in a single day. I was in San Francisco, the area and setting of Allen Ginsberg, and all about very modest poets were waking up prophets. I became sorely aware of how few poems I had written, and that these few had been finished at the latest three or four years earlier. Their style seemed distant, symbol-ridden and willfully difficult. I began to paraphrase my Latin quotations, and to add extra syllables to a line to make it clearer and more colloquial. I felt my old poems hid what they were really

about, and many times offered a stiff, humorless and even impenetrable surface. I am no convert to the "beats." I know well too that the best poems are not necessarily poems that read aloud. Many of the greatest poems can only be read to one's self, for inspiration is no substitute for humor, shock, narrative and a hypnotic voice, the four musts for oral performance. Still, my own poems seemed like prehistoric monsters dragged down into the bog and death by their ponderous armor. I was reciting what I no longer felt. What influenced me more than San Francisco and reading aloud was that for some time I had been writing prose. I felt that the best style for poetry was none of the many poetic styles in English, but something like the prose of Chekhov or Flaubert. When I returned to my home, I began writing lines in a new style.3)

This statement does not merely reveal Lowell's intention to break away from traditional poetic form; he underscores that the well-crafted verse form is inadequate for exploring his experiences to the greatest extent. Considering his old style, Lowell recognizes the way a prose style effects immediacy in the quest for past experiences.

In an interview with Frederick Seidel in 1961, Lowell expresses his admiration for Tolstoi's work: "his work is imagistic, it deals with all experience, and there seems to be no conflict of the form and content."4) He proceeds

---

3) Robert Lowell, "On 'Skunk Hour,'" *The Contemporary Poet as Artist and Critic*, ed. Anthony Ostroff (Boston: Little, Brown and Company, 1964) 108-9.

4) Frederick Seidel, "Interview with Robert Lowell," *Robert Lowell: A Portrait of the Artist in His Time*, ed. Robert Boyers (New York: David

to say that ". . . one thing is to get into poetry **that kind of human richness in rather simple descriptive language**"[5] (emphasis mine). In the same interview, asked whether he "intended to handle all that material in prose," Lowell replies:

> Yes. I found it got awfully tedious working out transitions and putting in things that didn't seem very important but were necessary to the prose continuity. Also, I found it hard to revise. Cutting it down into small bits, I could work on it much more carefully and make fast transitions. But there's another point about this mysterious business of prose and poetry, form and content, and the reasons for breaking forms. I don't think there's any very satisfactory answer. I seesaw back and forth between something highly metrical and something highly free; there isn't any one way to write. But it seems to me we've gotten into a sort of Alexandrian age. Poets of my generation and particularly younger ones have gotten terribly proficient at these forms. They write a very musical, difficult poem with tremendous skill, perhaps there's never been such skill. **Yet the writing seems divorced from culture somehow. It's become too much something specialized that can't handle much experience. It's a craft, purely a craft, and there must be some breakthrough back into life. Prose is in many ways better off than poetry.** It's quite hard to think of a young poet who has the vitality, say, of Salinger or Saul Bellow. Yet prose tends to very diffuse. The novel is really a much more difficult form than it seems; few people

---

Lewis, 1964) 267.

5) Frederick Seidel 267.

> have the wind to write anything that long. Even a short story demands almost poetic perfection. Yet on the whole prose is less cut off from life than poetry is. Now, some of this Alexandrian poetry is very brilliant, you would not have it changed at all. But I thought it was getting increasingly stifling. **I couldn't get my experience into tight metrical forms.**[6] (emphasis mine)

Here again, Lowell underlines the instrumental property of prose in delivering immediacy and continuity of experience. Metrical poetry, due to the inherent restrictions in its sound pattern, is inadequate to translate his experiences without break. Seen in light of this view of prose, then, Lowell's choice of prose for his autobiographical memoir is motivated by a desire to give a full confession of his past that would lead to a free exploration of the self. Lowell's abandonment of conventional poetic form to unconstrainedly investigate the past was like "playing tennis without a net."[7]

This prose memoir centers on the fragmented worlds of Lowell's parents as characterized by the constant friction between an intrusive mother and a listless, ineffectual father. More specifically, Lowell's father, Commander Lowell, is dispassionate, unenergetic, and irresolute, while his mother, Charlotte Winslow, is wayward, selfish, materialistic and vainglorious. Later on, this incompatibility, constituting a central plot in the prose sketch of his fam-

---

6) Frederick Seidel 269-70.

7) Take "My Last Afternoon with Uncle Devereux Winslow" for example. It was originally composed in prose, while finally revised in verse form.

ily, plays a decisive role in determining the fate of the young Lowell's self.

Interestingly enough, the personalities that Lowell's parents inherited, in part, from their ancestors anticipates the fragmented marital life of Commander Lowell and Charlotte Winslow. Early in the prose memoir, Lowell sketches the character of his paternal ancestors which was inherited by Commander Lowell:

> Bailey-Mason-Myers: Easy-going, Empire State patricians, these relatives of my Grandmother Lowell seemed to have given my father his character. For he likewise lacked that granite *back-countriness* which Grandfather Arthur Winslow attributed to his own ancestors, the iconoclastic mulish Dunbarton New Hampshire Starks. On the joint Mason-Myers bookplate, there are two merry and naked mermaids---lovely marshmallowy, boneless, Rubenseque butterballs, all burlesque-show bosoms and Flemish smile. Their motto, *malo frangere quam flectere*, read "I prefer to bend than to break." (*LS* 12, original italics)

The lack of "granite back-countriness" in the Lowells, the most conspicuous character of Lowell's ancestors on his father's side, leads to Commander Lowell's dissonance with his wife as well as to his repeated failure in his civilian career.

In contrast, Charlotte Winslow, Lowell's mother, was an overbearing and worldly woman. Her singular interest in money and her vanity persistently resulted in an antagonistic relationship with her husband. To satisfy her own selfish end, she unceasingly prompted her husband to resign from the navy and finally reduced him to an ineffectual person. The wilful Charlotte was the product of the materialistic, vainglorious Winslow whom Lowell blatantly attacks in his early poetry. Lowell seems to have resented particularly his maternal grandfather's dominance and influence over Charlotte even after her marriage.

As many critics point out, Lowell's early poems are concerned with the decline of religious faith which gave way to the growth of materialism. Hugh B. Staples, for example, remarks: "Like Eliot and Pound, Lowell is preoccupied with a sense of loss that results from contrasting the promise of the past to the futility of the present. The alienation of man from God, which I take to be the central theme of all the poems in *Land of Unlikeness*, finds its most dramatic expression from Lowell in the failure and death of the Puritan tradition."[8] In "Children of Light," for instance, Lowell describes the Pilgrim "fathers" as rigorous materialists:

> Our fathers wrung their bread from stocks and stones
> And fenced their gardens with the Redman's bones;
> Embarking from the Nether Land of Holland,
> Pilgrims unhouseled by Geneva's night,
> They planted here the Serpent's seeds of light;
> And here the pivoting searchlights probe to shock
> The riotous glass houses built on rock,
> And candles gutter by an empty altar,

---

8) Hugh B. Staples, *Robert Lowell: The First Twenty Years* (New York: Farrar, Straus and Cudahy, 1962) 28.

And light is where the landless blood of Cain
Is burning, burning the unburied grain.[9)]

Symbolically, Lowell embodies the Puritan fathers' spiritual emptiness and their greedy pursuit of wealth; since they were "unhoused by Geneva's night," the Pilgrim fathers planted "the Serpent's seed of light" in New England by disfiguring religious innocence. As the empty altar turned out hollow, religious piety vanished. Instead, the Puritan fathers multiplied violence and destruction, thus filling the new land with Cain's blood. As a result, the light here becomes ironical, because "the force of the Founding Fathers' religious zeal has been reduced to vain and illusory ritual."[10)]

Lowell's repugnance toward the descendents of the Puritan fathers is best expressed in "In Memory of Arthur Winslow" and "Mary Winslow." In particular, the former explicitly sets forth his contempt for his grandfather, his mother's lifelong idol. Although written in the form of elegy for his grandparents, both poems castigate the decayed religious values manifested in his grandparents. The first sequence of "In Memory of Arthur Winslow," "Death from Cancer" describes Arthur Winslow dying from cancer, which Lowell conceives as a symptom of modern capitalism:[11)]

---

9) Robert Lowell, *Lord Weary's Castle and The Mills of the Kavanaughs* (New York: Harcourt Brace Jovanovich Publishers, 1946) 34.

10) Hugh B. Staples 29.

11) For further, see Susan Sontag, *Illness as a Metaphor* (New York: Farrar, Straus and Giroux, 1978). In the book, examining illness which has been used as metaphors to indict a corrupt or unjust society, she sug-

This Easter, Arthur Winslow, less than dead,
Your people set you up in Phillips' House
To settle off your wrestling with the crab---
The claws drop flesh upon your yachting blouse.
Until longshoreman Charon come and stab
Through your adjusted bed
And crush the crab. On Boston Basin, Shells
Hit water by the Union Boat Club wharf:
You ponder why the coxes' squeakings dwarf
The resurrexit dominus of all the bells.[12)]

By putting Arthur Winslow in a specific locale, Lowell accentuates the degradation of religious faith in Boston. Although Arthur Winslow struggles against cancer ("wrestling with the crab") in Phillips' House, an expensive Massachusetts hospital, Lowell negates the possibility of resurrection by predicting the advent of Charon, a boatman who is known to ferry the souls of the dead across Acheron to the Hades. That is, Lowell shows that Arthur is so damned in religious terms that he is denied salva-

---

gests that tuberculosis and cancer are symptoms of capitalism: "Early capitalism assumes the necessity of regulated spending, saving, accounting, discipline---an economy that depends on the rational limitation of desire. TB is described in images that sum up the negative behavior of nineteenth-century *homo economicus*: consumption; wasting; squandering of vitality. Advanced capitalism requires expansion, speculation, the creation of new needs (the problem of satisfaction and dissatisfaction); buying on credit; mobility---an economy that depends on the irrational indulgence of desire. Cancer is described in images that sum up the negative behavior of twentieth-century homo economicus: abnormal growth; repression of energy, that is, refusal to consume or spend" (63).

12) *Lord Weary's Castle and The Mills of the Kavanaughs* 25.

tion after death.

In the second sequence, "Dunbarton," Lowell depicts the burial of Winslow. The decaying natural landscape suggests the dissolution of the initial religious faith of the Puritan fathers:

> The stones are yellow and the grass is gray
> Past Concord by the rotten lake and hill
> Where crutch and trumpet meet the limousine
> And half-forgotten Starks and Winslows fill
> The granite plot and the dwarf pines are green
> From watching for the day
> When the great year of the little yeomen come
> Bringing its landed Promise and the faith
> That made the Pilgrim Makers take a lathe
> And point their wooden steeples lest the Word be dumb.[13)]

To the family members of the Winslows and the Starks who come to the burial of Arthur Winslow with the support of crutch and trumpet, religious faith appears meaningless. Sermons here cannot be impressive: "The minister from Boston waves your shades." And the first selectman of Dunbarton honors the dead Winslow with "Wreaths of New Hampshire pine cones." All these funeral rites are underlined once again by Lowell's contemptuous conclusion: "The preacher's mouthings still/ Deafen my poor relations on the hill:/ their sunken landmarks echo what our fathers preached."

In the third sequence, "Five Years Later," more embit-

---

13) *Lord Weary's Castle and The Mills of the Kavanaughs* 26.

tered, Lowell strongly upbraids his grandfather's materialist expedition to the West, with an imitation of Mark Anthony's funeral oration in Shakespeare's *Julius Caesar*:

> I came to mourn you, not to praise the craft
> That netted you a million dollars, late
> Hosing out gold in Colorado's waste,
> Then lost it all in Boston real estate.[14)]

By telling us about the reputation which Arthur Winslow's ancestors achieved in American history, Lowell downgrades Winslow's materialistic search for gold in California.[15)] Here again, Lowell concludes the poem with the mocking statement that his grandfather was attracted to the capitalist crusade only by "devil's notions that your gold as least/ Could give back life to men who whipped or backed the King?"

In "Mary Winslow," Lowell censures his maternal

---

14) *Lord Weary's Castle and The Mills of the Kavanaughs* 27.

15) Jerome Mazzaro notes that Lowell's mother's side ancestors in the second stanza of "Five Years Later" made an outstanding contribution to the construction of the country: "The first is cited by the *Dictionary of American Biography* for his contributions to government as 'the first man to achieve success in England after receiving his training in affairs in America.' The second, for his contribution to art, as having been able with his other accomplishments 'to produce a quantity of fine silverwork, which for historical as well as esthetic reasons is among the silver most valued by American collectors.' The last, of his successes as a general: 'Oct. 4, 1777, he was promoted to the rank of brigadier-general in the Continental Service.' Thus, Lowell has stressed the contributions to government, art, and war which Winslow's ancestors have made." (15) See Jerome Mazzaro, *The Poetic Themes of Robert Lowell* (Ann Arbor: U of Michigan P, 1965) 14-15.

grandmother. Recalling his dying grandmother, Lowell harshly mocks her egocentricity which runs in her daughter Charlotte in "91 Revere Street" and "Sailing Home from Rapallo":

> Her Irish maids could never spoon out mush
> Or orange-juice enough; the body cools
> And smiles as a sick child
> Who adds up figures, and a hush
> Grips at the poised relations sipping sherry
> And tracking up the carpets of her four
> Room kingdom.[16)]

Short and simple, the description of Mary Winslow's deathbed scene is caustic and satiric. Compliment and sympathy for the dead person, essential elements of traditional elegy, are totally eliminated here; instead, the snobbishness of Mary, who demands fastidious care even at her deathbed is underlined. Though "Grandiloquent, square-jowled and worldly-wise,/ A Cleopatra in her housewife's dress,"[17)] death makes her pretentious life a mockery, much as her daughter's death in "Sailing Home from Rapallo" will point up the pretentions in her life.

As we have seen, Lowell is contemptuous of his maternal grandparents and those Bostonians who were responsible for the deterioration of Bostonian culture. Lowell's mother inherited all the values that Lowell attacks in his grandparents, and he regards her Winslow

---

16) *Lord Weary's Castle and The Mills of the Kavanaughs* 31.

17) *Lord Weary's Castle and The Mills of the Kavanaughs* 31.

values as the major source of her discord with his father as well as of his own victimization as a child. In some sense, "91 Revere Street" examines Lowell's victimization which originates in the cultural dissipation of his grandparents and his mother.

To show further how the self is entrapped in those familial clashes, Lowell looks beyond the world of his grandparents and charts the antithetical world of his parents. Though married to Commander Lowell, Lowell's mother still enshrined her father Arthur Winslow as the Napoleon of her life. Thus, she had neither respect for nor marital commitment to her husband; further, she was resentful of her husband's lack of charismatic quality: "She [Lowell's mother] had been married nine or ten years and still suspected that her husband was savorless, unmasterful, merely considerate" (*LS* 18). Lowell goes on to describe his mother's critique of his father:

> Unmasterful---Father's specialized efficiency lacked utterly the flattering bossiness she so counted on from her father, my Grandfather Winslow. It was not Father's absence on sea-duty that mattered; it was the eroding necessity of moving with him, of keeping in step. . . . Fully conscious of her uniqueness and normality she basked in the refreshing stimulation of dreams in which she imagined Father as suitably sublimed. She used to describe such a sublime man to me over tea and English muffins. He was Siegfried carried lifeless through the shining air by Brunnhilde to Valhalla, and accompanied by the throb of my Great Aunt Sarah playing his leitmotif in the released manner taught her by the Abbe Liszt.

> Or Mother's hero dove through the grottoes of the Rhine and slaughtered the homicidal and vulgar dragon coiled about the golden hoard. Mother seemed almost light-headed when she retold the romance of Sarah Bernhardt in L'Aiglon, the Eaglet, the weakling! She would speak the word weakling with such amused vehemence that I formed a grandiose and false image of L'Agilon's Father, the big Napoleon: he was a strong man who scratched under his paunchy little white vest a torso all hair, muscle, and manliness. (*LS* 18, original italics)

As metonymically illustrated, Arthur Winslow, to Mother, is more than father: hero, idol, and lover. Her father still keeps her heart where, as a husband, Commander Lowell ought to be. Thus, her marriage to Commander Lowell is nothing but a physical union because her world is still occupied by her father even after marriage. Actually, their marriage was loveless from the start. Arthur Winslow, who "espoused a brand of New England integrity that even hard-line Bostonians considered somewhat over-rhetorical and Prussian,"[18] was very strict and rigorous about his daughter's suitors, which is described in "During Fever": "Mother, you smile/ as if you saw your Father/ inches away yet hidden, as when he groused behind a screen/ over a National Geographic Magazine,/ whenever young men came to court you" (*LS* 80). After rejecting a number of suitors, he decided to accept Bob Lowell only due to the "historical appropriateness" of the

18) Ian Hamilton, *Robert Lowell: A Biography* (New York: Random House, 1982) 4.

Lowells. Once he became aware of the name of the family, Arthur ignored rumors about Bob's character. Ian Hamilton, Lowell's biographer, remarks that Bob's submissive character pleased both father and daughter: "Arthur Winslow was not looking to be replaced as the dominant figure in his favorite daughter's life. Nor was Charlotte herself in need of any extra restraints upon her own natural bossiness. She had a man she worshipped; now she wanted one who would unquestioningly worship her. For both father and daughter, Bob's combination of weak character and strong lineage was indeed perfectly correct."[19)]

All of this biographical information suggests that Lowell's mother internalized her father's world in many respects, a world Lowell unfailingly condemns. Like her father, first of all, she is an enthusiastic materialist; for example, she arduously clings to her family inheritance:

> Cousin Cassie only became a close relation in 1922. In that year she died. After some unpleasantness between Mother and a co-heiress, Helen Bailey, the estate was divided. Mother used to return frozen and thrilled from her property disputes. . . . Shortly after our move to Boston in 1924, a score of unwanted Myers portraits was delivered to our new house on Revere Street. These were later followed by "their dowry"---four moving vans groaning with heavy Edwardian Furniture. My father began to receive his first quarterly payments from the Mason-Myers Julian-James Trust Fund, sums "not grand

19) Ian Hamilton 5.

> enough to corrupt us," Mother explained, "but sufficient to prevent Daddy from being entirely at the mercy of his salary." (*LS* 13)

Commander Lowell's salary fails to satisfy her vanity and meet her version of a well-provided life.

The following passage, a sketch of Mother's interior decoration, shows a taste for beauty that depicts her shaky and precarious life, a life that closely sums up the Winslow family:

> Mother's comfort was chic, romantic, impulsive. If her sliver service shone, it shone with hectic perfection to rebuke the functional domesticity of naval wives. She had determined to make her *ambiance* beautiful and luxurious, but wanted neither her beauty not her luxury unaccompanied. Beauty pursued too exclusively meant artistic fatuity of a kind made farcical by her Aunt Sarah Stark Winslow, a beauty too lofty and original ever to marry, a prima donna on the piano, too high-strung ever to give a public recital. Beauty alone meant the maudlin ignominy of having one's investments managed by interfering relatives. Luxury alone, on the other hand, meant for Mother the "paste and fool's-gold polish" that one met with in the foyer of the new Statler Hotel. She loathed the "undernourishment" of Professor Burckhard's Bauhaus modernism, yet in moments of pique she denounced our pompous Myers mahoganies as: "suitable for politicians at the Bellevue Hotel." She kept a middle-of-the-road position, and much admired Italian pottery with its fresh peasant colors and puritanical, clean-cut lines. She was fond of saying, "The French do have

> taste," but spoke with a double-edged irony which implied the French, with no moral standards to support their finish, were really no better than naval yahoos. Mother's beautiful house was dignified by a rich veneer of the useful.[20] (*LS* 33-34, original italics)

Although Mother hates Aunt Sarah's neurotic notion of beauty, the definition of her taste comes close to Aunt Sarah's: "a beauty too lofty and original ever to marry, a prima donna on the piano, too high-strung ever to give a public recital." Indeed, her effort to "make her *ambiance* beautiful and luxurious" only results in confusion. Mother's assumption that her aesthetics, combined with beauty and luxury, wins *via media* turns out implausible. All that remains with Mother is the Italian pottery with "puritanical clean-out lines" which represents nothing but coldness and fragility. In light of her version of beauty, it is not surprising that Mother, quite anxious about refined beauty in her, finds everything concerning the navy abominable: "Mother hated the Navy, hated naval society, naval pay, and the trip-hammer rote of settling and unsettling a house every other year when Father was transferred to a new station of ship" (*LS* 18). And her infatuation with refinement even makes her hypersensitive about the address of her house: "We are barely perched on the outer rim of the hub of decency" (*LS* 15).

Like her mother, Mary Winslow, described as calling

---

20) In the selection of passages concerning Mother's interior decoration and Father's den and in understanding the symbols, I am much indepted to Marjorie G. Perloff. For further details, see *The Poetic Art of Robert Lowell* (Ithaca: Cornell UP, 1973) 94-98.

constant care even at her death bed in "Mary Winslow," Lowell's mother yearns for exclusive attention from people:

> Our Sunday dinner guests were often naval officers. Naval officers were not Mother's sort; very few people were her sort in those days, and that was her trouble---a very authentic, human, and plausible difficulty, which made Mother's life one of much suffering. She needed to feel liked, admired, surrounded by the approved and familiar. Her haughtiness and chillness came from apprehension. She would start talking like a *grande dame* and then stand back rigid and faltering, as if she feared being crushed by her own massively intimidating offensive. (*LS* 32, original italics)

But unlike the confident Mary Winslow, Mother's love of worldly goods and haughtiness is accompanied by inner fear. Lowell sees her as the perverse product of the debased features of New England Puritanism which, to surmount temptation, repudiates pleasures of the flesh, and embraces hard work and frugality---a "worldly asceticism" which Max Weber views as the fundamental source of the birth of capitalism.[21)]

Lowell's father is totally contrasted with his mother in many respects. Unlike other branches of the Lowell family which were wealthy, the family into which Commander Lowell was born was better known for its contributions to American history:[22)]

---

21) Max Weber, *The Protestant Ethic and the Spirit of Capitalism,* trans. Talcott Parsons (New York: Scribners, 1930) 95-154.

> Bob was from the poor. . . . branch of the Lowells---priests and poets figured prominently among his immediate forebears. James Russell Lowell was a great-great-uncle and Robert Traill Spence Lowell I, James Russell's elder brother, was moderately well known for his verses and for a novel, *The New Priest in Conception Bay*. The Lowell millions, though, were elsewhere, with the bankers and the lawyers and cotton magnates: cousins all, but hardly intimates, and in a quite separate financial league. From the late eighteenth century, the Traill/Spence line of Lowells had been the pious poor relations, admired their good. . . . works, but viewed as somehow quirkily irrelevant to the main thrust of the Lowell enterprise. Bob's feebleness, for instance, would have been seen by "real" Lowells as the to-be-expected outcome of four generations of worship and word-spinning.[23)]

In this branch of his father's family, there was no conspicuously hard-line capitalist like those associated with the dissipated Puritan ideals Lowell condemned in his early poetry. As a result, Lowell cannot denounce his paternal ancestors for materialistic passion, he highlights the lack of "granite back-countriness" as the salient shortcoming of his paternal ancestors.

In contrast to his wife, Commander Lowell was in-

---

22) This is not to say that the Winslows were not prominent in the political, military, and cultural history of America. As mentioned earlier, some of the Winslows left considerable mark in the founding history of America. Yet it is true that the Lowells contribution to America is much more remarkable than the Winslows.

23) Ian Hamilton 6.

clined to submit rather than to resist or to assert, a trait he seems to have inherited from his ancestor Mordecai Myers. Reluctant to trust his own experiences and judgement, he rested upon statistics: "He was deep---not with profundity, but with the dumb depth of one who trusted in statistics and was dubious of personal experience" (*LS* 17). Two things stood out in his life: his temperament was the direct opposite of his wife's, and his career was marked by repeated failures and humiliations. Lowell's portrayal of his father's den illustrates how ordinary and impractical Commander Lowell was:

> The walls of Father's minute Revere Street den-parlor were bare and white. His bookshelves were bare and white. The den's one adornment was a ten-tube home-assembled battery radio set, whose loudspeaker had the shape and color of a Mexican sombreto. The radio's specialty was getting programs from Australia and New Zealand in the early hours of the morning.
>
> My father's favorite piece of den furniture was his oak and "rhinoceros hide" armchair. It was ostentatiously a masculine, or rather a bachelor's chair. It had a notched, adjustable back; it was black, cracked, hacked, scratched, splintered, gouged, initialed, gunpowder-charred and tumbler-ringed. It looked like pale tobacco leaves laid on dark tobacco leaves. I doubt if Father, a considerate man, was responsible for any of the marring. The chair dated from his pleb days at the Naval Academy, and had been bought from a shady, shadowy, roaring character, midshipman 'Beauty' Burford. Father loved each disfigured inch. (*LS* 17)

Though simple, Father's den abounds with trifling trinkets which mirror his lackadaisical life. Above all, Lowell's repeated use of the adjectives "bare and white" for bookshelves and walls intensifies the man's lack of interest in beauty or luxury, two things that govern his wife's lifelong dream.[24] The items in Father's den attest to the owner's listless personality. As Marjorie Perloff points out, for example, his radio's specialty, picking up radio program from Australia and New Zealand, does not seem to be relevant to his career, past and present. His furniture, his "rhinoceros hide" armchair, only reveals Commander's meaningless preservation of his former career.[25] For the armchair, purchased from "a shady, shadowy, roaring character, midshipman 'Beauty' Burford," has nothing to do with any heroic acts of Commander Lowell as a naval officer. The chair loses its prime gloss, but it is still loved by the owner perhaps only because it is "ostentatiously a masculine, or rather a bachelors chair." But the chair's physical decay may suggest his father's gradual loss of manhood.

As the totally contrasted Winslow/Lowell worlds show, the clash between the couple cannot be resolved easily. Commander Lowell has not experienced heroic combat as a naval officer; he has neither an affection for the navy nor self-esteem, but will not resign. His lack of resolution hinders him from leaving the navy and satisfying his wife. But since Mrs. Lowell is impatient and detests the navy,

---

24) Marjorie G. Perloff 97.

25) Marjorie G. Perloff 97.

she decides to buy "the squalid, impractical Revere Street house" to avoid "naval yards, steam, and 'the fellows'" (*LS* 18). Obviously, this purchase is made without consulting with her husband, a clear sign of her disrespect for Commander Lowell who thereby loses face in front of his superior: "He [Admiral De Stahl] was outraged, stormed about 'flaunting private fortunes in the face of naval tradition,' and ordered my father to sleep on bounds at the Yard in the house provided for that purpose" (*LS* 23).

After they move to new house on Revere Street, disagreements between the couple become frequent and turbulent. To satisfy her family, Lowell's mother repeatedly urges her husband to resign from the navy to earn more money in a civilian career: "'A *man* must make up his *own* mind. Oh Bob, if you are going to resign, do it *now* so that I can at least plan for your son's *survival* and education on a single continent'" (*LS* 19-20, original italics). But for no particular reason Commander Lowell hesitates. As a result, friction between the couple mounts until, at last, she gives him an ultimatum; "One night she said with murderous coolness, 'Bobby and I are leaving for papá's'" (*LS* 19). The young Lowell himself recalls the clashes in pain: "91 Revere Street was the setting for those arthritic spiritual pains that troubled us for the two years my mother spent in trying to argue my father into resigning from the Navy" (*LS* 19).

At this time, the central point in the continuous discord between the Lowells was whether Commander Lowell should resign from the navy for a better-paying civilian job. The problem intensified Commander Lowell's diffidence and strengthened his wife's resolve: "I could often hear actual words. 'Yes, yes, yes,' Father would mumble. He was 'backsliding' and 'living in the fool's paradise of habitual retarding and retarded do-nothing inertia.' Mother had violently set her heart on the resignation" (*LS* 19).

When Commander Lowell eventually gives in to his wife's long wishes, he produced unseemly excuses to gain approval from a colleague:

> . . . "Billy boy, it's a darned shame, but this State of Massachusetts doesn't approve of the service using its franchise and voting by mail. I haven't had a chance to establish residence since our graduation on '07. I think I'll put my blues in mothballs and become a *cit* just to prove I still belong to the country. The directors of Lever Brothers' Soap in Cambridge . . . I guess for *cits*, Billy, they've really got something on the ball, because they tell me they want me on their team." (*LS* 42, original italics)

This resignation evokes an insult from his fellow officer Billy Harkness, so much "a man of action" that he even confronts Mother: "'Why in God's name should a man with Bob's brilliant cerebellum go and mess up his record by actually *begging* for that impotent field nigger's job of second in command at the defunct Boston Yard'"(*LS* 45-46, original italics). Commander Lowell's defeat at his wife's hands and humiliation from his friend aroused in the young Lowell anger as well as compassion (*LS* 42-46). To the young Lowell, this became a crucial moment of loss: loss of a role model on which to fashion his own identity. Lowell recalls the intense humiliation at his father's submissiveness: "Those dinners, those apologies! Perhaps I exaggerate their embarrassment because they hover so grayly in recollection and seem to anticipate ominously my father's downhill progress as a civilian and Bostonian" (*LS* 43).

While Lowell is disappointed by his father, it is anger that his mother draws from him. She drives his father toward becoming a nonentity, and she tries to control the young Lowell himself. Such an overbearing Mother adversely affects the development of Lowell's identity. In another prose piece "Antebellum Boston," for instance, Lowell describes how his mother hindered the proper growth of his personality by attempting to impose her own predilections on him:

> When I was convalescing from flu, Christmas holidays arrived and I associated in my mind the lazy, indulgent recovering days with actual calendar holidays. Father was away at sea and Grandfather Winslow made us a surprise visit from Boston. My father sent me a big bundle of toys and in my self-concentration I thought I had the toys only because Father was away, and so his absence seemed delightful. When he returned, I ran up to him with tears in my eyes and said, "Daddy, I love you, but please go away again so that Santa can mail us a wagon-load of toys." Father seemed rather queasy in the face of this demonstration from his son.
>
> The toys had been chosen with the notion of impressing upon me the glamour of Father's naval career

> by comparison with mere civilian life and parenthood. . . . Among my gifts was a grim, gray wooded model of a German U-boat. By pressing a button, I could snap a trap-like spring inside the U-boat which made its gear collapse on the carpet, as though the thing had been hit by a depth bomb. This device was meant to teach children that wars meant business and, further, it was the very magic of toy itself. I was dismayed when Mother snatched my prize from me, disemboweled it of its spring, and then returned it, a miserable, weightless, warped wreak of its former war-like self.[26)]

As Lowell describes, his mother endeavored to estrange him from his father. Aware of his wife's attempt to monopolize his son, Commander Lowell became embarrassed at young Lowell's affection toward him. As the toy episode shows, his mother intervened, determined to exclude everything about the husband's profession from the young Lowell. By disemboweling the toy that signifies war (the Navy), Mother removed the father who might claim the young Lowell, thereby controlling the young Lowell's self. In a sense, the mother's action is an effort on her part to incarcerate the young Lowell's self into her world.[27)]

---

26) Robert Lowell, "Antebellum Boston," *Collected Prose*, ed. Robert Giroux (New York: Farrar, Straus and Giroux, 1987) 305.

27) The toy episode in "Antebellum Boston," which was written in 1957, must have made quite an impression on Lowell as a boy. The episode appears in a different version in an unpublished manuscript: "This is my first remembered meeting with my grandfather, and I know that it was my birthday because I see him standing beside a present from my father, a flotilla of little camouflaged wooden warships that had been

But his mother's attempt to control him arouses Lowell's resistance in many episodes of "91 Revere Street." Despite her sustained hindrance, Lowell seeks to establish a masculine identity in himself. This is underlined by the fact that the young Lowell wants to identify with his father, even as he is, at the same time, angry with his father. The young Lowell finds himself entangled in psychological problem, because he cannot find a role model from which to consolidate his self.

At the beginning of the prose memoir, Lowell confesses that he is fascinated by the romantic figure of his great-great-father on his father's side, Major Mordecai Myers:

---

laid out along the mantelpiece. They had been purchased in the name of, and as a tribute to my father who was off on sea-duty. Like later presents from my father, these toys had been bought with considerable pains and were a remarkable bargain, and very unfeminine. Made in Japan the boats were outrageously anti-German: the best boat was an American hos[pi]tal ship magnif[i]cently marked with warning red crosses. By pressing a button on a cord, a concealed spring mouse-trapped shut and the cabins and turrets of the hospital ship collapsed on the floor---it had been hit by submarine's torpedo. However, the toy was meant for adults and my mother soon robbed it of all allure. She snatched it from my hands, disembowelled it of its dangerous spring, and then gave its back, weightless and harmless, and an insipid husk of its former warlike outrages" (Witek 719). Terri Witek considers Mother's action here as symbolical "castrating," and Father, she continues to say, is getting away from the powerful center (Witek 716). For further, see Terri Witek, "Robert Lowell's Tokens of the Self," *American Literature* 63 (1991): 712-26. And for further detail about the toy episode quoted in this chapter, see Robert Lowell, "Antebellum Boston," *Collected Prose*, 291-308.

> Undoubtedly Major Mordecai had lived in a more ritualistic, gaudy, and animal world than twentieth-century Boston. There was something undecided, Mediterranean, versatile, almost double-faced about his bearing which suggested that, even to his contemporaries, he must have seemed gratuitously both *ce-devant* and *parvenu*. He was a dark man, a German Jew---no downright Yankee, but maybe such a fellow as Napoleon's mad, pomaded son-of-an-innkeeper-general, Junot, Duc D'Abrantes; a man like mad George III's pomaded, disreputable son, "Prinny," the Prince Regent. Or he was one of those Moorish-l ooking dons painted by his contemporary, Goya---some leader of Spanish guerrillas against Bonaparte's occupation, who fled to South America. Our Major's suffering almond eye rested on his luxurious dawn-colored fingers ruffling an off-white glove. (*LS* 11-12)

Major Mordecai Myers' impression on the young Lowell seems so great that he takes delight in collecting toy soldiers and memorizing the name of French generals. Yet after Lowell becomes aware that Mordecai was only a civilian soldier, his affection for the major disappears. And, when the young Lowell comes to know that his father is subservient to his wife and his friends, then his father as a center for his emerging self loses credibility. Marjorie Perloff describes the position of the complicated self of the young Lowell: Lowell puts "his childhood self in the center of a triangle at whose apex is the romantic figure of his ancestor, Major Mordecai Myers . . . and whose base has two points, his father and mother, figures equally lifeless and futile, but strangely unlike each other and constantly at war."[28] As the prose memoir progresses, the young Lowell gradually grows disenchanted with his earlier romantic dream of his ancestors. But the disenchantments do not lead to a clarification of self; rather, Lowell becomes confused at the surrounding reality and develops a complex psychological condition; that is, he revolts and rebels against his mother, a point that tells us that Lowell naturally hates his grandfather. Jay Martin points out that Lowell's condemnation of his grandfather includes "an attack on Winslow's daughter---Lowell's mother."[29] Strangely enough, however, he takes his maternal grandfather, the Napoleon of his mother, as the role model: "A ray of hope in the far future was my white-haired Grandfather Winslow, whose unchecked commands and demands were always upsetting people for their own good---he was all I could ever want to be: the bad boy, the problem child, the commodore of his household" (*LS* 28). But Lowell's attraction to his maternal grandfather, only linked with his rebellion against his parents, cannot be considered as a sudden expression of love for him.

Lowell comes to find his identity where power is located. Particularly, Lowell's experience at home and in Brimmer breeds in the young Lowell gender confusion:

> *Boy*---at that time this word had private associations for

28) Marjorie Perloff 94.

29) Jay Martin, "Grief and Nothingness: Loss and Mourning in Lowell's Poetry," *Robert Lowell: Essays on the Poetry*, eds. Steven Gould Axelrod and Helen Deese (New York: Cambridge UP, 1986) 32.

> me; it meant weakness, outlawry, and yet was a status to be held onto. Boys were a sideline at my Brimmer School. The eight superior grades were limited to girls. In these grades, moreover, scholarship was made subservient to discipline, as if in contempt of the male's two idols: career and earning power. The school's tone, its ton, was a blend of the feminine and the military, a bulky reality governed in turn by stridency, smartness, and steadiness. The girls wore white jumpers, black skirts, stockings and rectangluar low-heeled shoes. (*LS* 25)

Brimmer was not only "a blend of the feminine and the military" (*LS* 25); it was "entirely a woman's world" which is "ruled by woman's obvious aims and by her naive pragmatism" (*LS* 27). As Hamilton points out, Lowell "identified the regime of Brimmer with the regime of 91 Revere Street" because both were "worlds ruled by women"[30]: "I wished I were an older girl. I wrote Santa Claus for field hockey stick. To be a boy at Brimmer was to be small, denied and weak" (*LS* 27). Such a confused recognition indicates that for the young Lowell, women are "more powerful than men."[31] Interestingly, the confused feeling leads him to hostility rather than affection toward women and his friends. Despite his aggressiveness, however, Lowell is "reduced to a version of femaleness rather than lifted to masculinity by this role model."[32] Undeniably, this reversed personality gives rise to perplexed behavior as well as to a stunted development of

30) Ian Hamilton 15.

31) Jay Martin 28.

32) Terri Witek 719.

the self. For instance, Lowell became contemptuous of a fellow student, Elie Norton, when she embarrassed herself and became incontinent at school. Lowell's behavior toward his best friend Eric was unstable and erratic. When, due to his own fault, they quarrel, Lowell behaves aggressively toward Eric. Though his own manners are untidy, he fails to overlook slovenly behavior in others. Bent on rebelling against his mother, Lowell is driven into unreasonable postures. For example, when he learns of his mother's jealousy of the Burckhard family, he decides to like them more than ever: "I admired the Burckhards and felt at home in their house, and these feelings were only intensified when I discovered that my mother was always ill at ease with them" (*LS* 21).

Aspiring to an identity, Lowell rebels against his mother's exercise of authority in any form. One Christmas Eve when Commander Lowell was suddenly called by his superior to naval duty, his mother rushed to her son's bedroom and said, hugging him: "Oh Bobby, it's such a comfort to have a man in the house" (*LS* 24). To this, the young Lowell responded in sheer spite: "I am not a man," "I am a boy" (*LS* 24). This response, to use Jay Martin's term, is "a set of contradictions: He idealized but feared his mother, while he depreciated but secretly admired his father."[33)]

Mother, intrusive and repressive, incarcerates her husband and the young Lowell in her world. Yet she does not recognize that it is she who prevents her husband

---

33) Jay Martin 28.

from becoming "a man."[34] Father, originally mild, gradually turned into an ineffectual person by his overbearing wife, and thus completely lost his dignity and respect. Although the young Lowell endeavors to seek his identity, he loses idols (role model) in the family one by one: Major Mordecai Myers and his father. Like Father, the young Lowell himself becomes emasculated and incarcerated in his mother's world. Mother's complete domination in 91 Revere Street is almost tantamount to a metaphorical divorce, thus reducing the young Lowell to a psychological orphan. Yet this is not to say that Mother's triumph alone leads to Lowell's divided self. Father, passively emasculated, also contributes to the division by preventing the development of the young Lowell's self. For example, when Lowell remembers his father who makes slim excuses even to his old friends for his resignation from the navy, Lowell's anger and pity for his father comes to its culmination: "Those dinners, those apologies! Perhaps I exaggerate their embarrassment because they hover so grayly in recollection and seem to anticipate ominously my father's downhill progress as a civilian and Bostonian" (*LS* 43). That is to say, the embattled parents are responsible for the complicated self in Lowell.

For Lowell, the divisions in his own self and in his family, as well as those in society at large mirror one another. The disintegration of one is also its disintegration of the others, and the condition of one becomes the

34) Marjorie G. Perloff 96.

text for understanding the condition of the rest. The wrecked dream of the Beacon Hill couple is one such text:

> "A woman works from sun to sun," he [Father] said, "but a sailor's watch is never done." He compared a naval officer's hours with a doctor's, hinted at surprise maneuvers, and explained away the uncommunicative arrogance of Admiral De Stahl: "The Old Man has to be hush-hush." Later that night, I lay in bed and tried to imagine that my father was leading his engineering force on a surprise maneuver through arctic wastes. A forlorn hope! "Hush-hush, hush-hush," whispered the snowflakes as big as street lamps as they broke on Father---broke and buried. Outside, I heard real people singing carols, shuffling snow off their shoes, opening and shutting doors. I worried at the meaning of a sense I had heard quoted from the *Boston Evening Transcript*: "On this Christmas Eve, as usual, the whole Beacon Hill can be expected to become a single old-fashioned open house---the names of mine host the Hill, and her guests will read like the contents of the social Register." I imagined Beacon Hill changed to the snow queen's palace, as vast as the north pole. My father pressed a cold finger to his lip: "hush-hush," and led his surprise squad of sailors around an alter, but the altar was a tremendous cash register, whose roughened nickel surface was cheaply decorated with trowels, pyramids, and Arabic swirls. A great drawer helplessly chopped back and forth, unable to shut because choked with greenbacks. (*LS* 23-24)

This passage symbolically draws upon, as well as unites,

the breakdown of the Beacon Hill mother's dream and Lowell's own dream of Commander. As we have seen, although the young Lowell places father figures like Modecai Myers and his own father Commander Lowell at the center of his self, he becomes disenchanted with them. Like his father's failure as civilian, the Beacon Hill mother's dream also fails. On the individual level, this broken dream reflects the distorted identity of the young Lowell; on the level of American history, the failed dream, which Lowell's picture describes, signifies the wreckage of the American dream.

The primary plot of Lowell's autobiography centers around an unbridgeable gulf that opens between wife and husband. The irreconciliability of the antagonistic character ends with no sure sense of the self available to the young Lowell. The sensitive young Lowell thinks and behaves under the influence of those nearest him, his family. As M. L. Rosenthal notes, "The emotional difficulties of the adults around him, their passions and failures, their exciting habits of speech are the meat upon which his intense inwardness feeds."[35] Lowell's Revere Street house represents, indeed, incorporates the young Lowell's humiliation, resentment against his parents and his warped personality. The worn furniture in the Revere Street house is a metonym for not just the devastation of the Lowells, but also the deprivation of the young Lowell's self.

"91 Revere Street" recalls and analyzes the two closed

---

35) M. L. Rosenthal 39.

worlds of Father and Mother. Questing archaeologically into the past, Lowell charts the essential conflict of the two discrete worlds, and suggests the fate of his own identity as engendered by two such closed worlds. By conducting a dialogue with the past, Lowell not merely reflects on the past experiences but analyzes the self-fragmentation which results from the sheer difference between his two different parents. Thus, Lowell's recollection of "rocklike" thing in the past is an attempt to understand his present; in terms of structure of *Life Studies*, this prose memoir opens a chapter for the following dialogue.

Chapter 4

The Self Remapped in the Family

Maurice Merleau-Ponty says: "The world is not what I think, but what I live through. I am open to the world, I have no doubt that I am in communication with it, but I do not possess it; it is inexhaustible."[1)] Our being in the world, according to him, entails communication with others, and this reciprocal interaction between ourselves and the world yields a transformation in ourselves. The self, if it is in communication with the world, must be in flux and alter itself incessantly. The fourth part of *Life Studies* shows that there is neither an independent self

1) Maurice Merleau-Ponty, *Phenomenology of Perception* xvi-xvii.

nor a fixed self which is free of the world. That is to say, the possibilities of the self are closely bound up with those of the world. Lowell's journey into his family leads him to understand his family members and helps shape new relations between them and himself. As a matter of fact, the prose autobiography, the second part of *Life Studies*, focuses on the young Lowell's self shattered by the circumstances of his family. In "91 Revere Street," Lowell quests for the origin of his own alienation in order to understand his present. The young Lowell's self in the prose, characterized by a conflict owing to the polarized personalities in his parents, is now on its way to a reconstruction. Rather than the self and the world, the first section of the fourth part presents the self in the world, which, by fusing different experiences, moves on to maturity. As the fourth part progresses, Lowell gradually transforms his view of his family, and his self in the family poems of the fourth part changes into reconciliation with his family members.

The opening poem, "My Last Afternoon with Uncle Devereux Winslow," which records Lowell's self in flux, prefigures a possibility of Lowell's altered relationship with his family. In "My Last Afternoon," Lowell pushes his imagination back to his childhood and corresponds to the past in terms of the young Lowell's perception. The whole poem is narrated through a young boy's perception of his grandfather's farm. As the poem proceeds, what the young Lowell finds there is something horrifying and painful. When the poem arrives at its end, the boy's perception turns to the recognition of mortality in the world.

That is, Lowell comes to know what the outer world harbors: death, decay, and renewal. Such an awareness generates self-transformation in the poet.

Unlike "91 Revere Street," "My Last Afternoon" avoids setting up a contrast between the two distinct families: rather than denouncing the Winslows, Lowell as a boy extols grandfather's farm as the most delightful place: "Nowhere was anywhere after a summer/ at my Grandfather's farm." Lowell's presentation of his poignant rebellion against his parents at the beginning of the poem shows how much the young Lowell is fascinated by his grandfather's world: " 'I won't go with you. I want to stay with Grandpa!'/ That's how I threw cold water/on my Mother and Father's/ watery martini pipe dreams at Sunday dinner." Needless to say, this fascination comes from a young boy's perception of the world, and the young Lowell gradually loses his initial sentiment of the Winslows.

Since Lowell as a boy perceives grandfather's world on the surface, he does not seem to be disturbed at all by what he sees:

> snapshots of his *Liberty Bell* silver mine;
> his high school at *Stukkert am Neckar*:
> stogie-brown beams; fools'-gold nuggets;
> octagonal red tiles,
> sweaty with a secret dank, crummy with ant-stale;
> a Rocky Mountain chaise longue,
> its legs, shellacked saplings.
> A pastel-pale Huckleberry Finn
> fished with a broom straw in a basin

hollowed out of a millstone.
Like my Grandfather, the décor
was manly, comfortable,
overbearing, disproportioned. (*LS* 60)

The "works of my Grandfather's hands" are so boyish as to appeal to a child. To the boy, they are all attractive. As metonyms, these details represent Lowell's grandfather's house and his way of life. The pictures record grandfather's expedition to the West and his education in Germany, the overbearing period of grandfather's life. But we find that the legs of the "Rocky Mountain chaise" have lost the originally applied varnish; that "Huckleberry Finn," though "fished with a broom straw in a basin/ hollowed out of a millstone," also becomes "pastel-pale." The closing lines sum up Lowell's grandfather's world: "manly, comfortable, overbearing"; yet his grandfather's world turns out "disproportioned."

The appearance of Sadie and Nellie at sunset, "bearing pitchers of ice-tea/ oranges, lemons, mint, and peppermints,/ and the jug of shandygaff," sets forth a picture of lovely farm, yet followed by an implication of "the inherent futility of the Edwardian elegance."[2] Particularly, the name of the farm, artificially coined as "*Char-de-sa*," appears to be permanent and pompous, but it merely accentuates Grandfather Winslow's "disproportioned" world which seems hollow. By recalling the deceased "Cinder, our Scottie puppy" and by placing the boy who sits "mixing black earth and lime," symbolic of knowledge of

2) Marjorie G. Perloff 148.

life and death, the closing lines of the first section foreshadow the young Lowell's recognition of the world which comes in the end of the poem.[3)]

---

3) The symbolic meaning of earth and lime, the most significant recurring motif, has prompted a number of different interpretations. Hugh Staples takes the two elements as death: "Both elements suggest death; the black earth, normally a symbol of fertility and growth is cool; the white lime has only the heat of dissolution and decay; mixed together, as the farmer cementing a root-house is doing, they solidify into one permanent, rocklike aggregate, as Uncle Devereux Winslow's body is to do in its ultimate metamorphosis" (Staples 78). Jerome Mazzaro, connecting "a pile of black earth" and "a pile of lime" with the actions of the entire book, accounts for the whole structure of *Life Studies*: "The structure of the poem follows the time-shift technique and concentrates on the tension and on the incidental observations of Lowell playing, his hands first on a pile of earth and then on a pile of lime. There is no single illumination to be drawn from the observations. Rather, the pictorial effect, suggestive of the "life studies" title of the section, lies in a patterning of metaphors of earth, water, sky, death, and stone" (Mazzaro 111). According to Mazzaro, the previous image of the Winslows changes in terms of the patterning of the metaphor: "Formerly, actions had painted Winslows above the usual cut of man in heroic poses. Now their actions blend like the earth, lime, and water into deathly rocklike shapes. In these shapes the Winslows are imaged, and the remaining poems in the first part of the section complete the images thus begun"(Mazzaro 111). Stephen Yenser says: "Black earth, popularly regraded as fertile soil, is patently symbolic life; while lime, an extremely caustic substance which in one of its forms is used to destroy the bodies of dead farm stock, is just as obviously symbolic of death. The young Lowell's mixing of earth and lime, then, reflects the crucial situation, in which the process of living is most clearly identifiable with that of dying"(Yenser 138). Discussing the uncle's death in the closing lines of the poem, Yenser elaborates again on the symbol: "the process [of life and death] terrifies the young Lowell, for it makes him see for the first time that his life entails his death, that living and dying can be synonymous; and this realization makes him yearn for flight into a realm where things are immutable and perfect, where

Section II sketches the young Lowell's vision of dream and reality. The boy, wearing "formal pearl gray short," envisions immortality: "My perfection was the Olympian/ poise of my models in the imperishable autumn/ display windows/ of Rogers Peet's boy's store . . ." But all that Lowell as a boy shows is only that the dream of perfection is not durable, especially in the face of reality, by adding that the "formal pearl gray shorts" were worn only for three minutes as well as by contrasting the brief illusion with an actual place name---"Rogers Peet's boys' store below the State House/ in Boston." Because it is in incessant movement, Lowell suggests, the reality, though displeasing, cannot be avoided: "Distorting drops of water/ pinpricked my face in the basin's mirror."

Part III specifies the inexorable reality of change with a sketch of the life-in-death of Aunt Sarah. Although Aunt Sarah in her twenties "tilted her archaic Athenian nose/ and jilted an Astor," she has dwindled into a neurotic performer on a "dummy piano" instead of a Symphony Hall pianist. Aunt Sarah "rises like the phoe-

---

there is only 'the one color'; and, finally, the force of this realization accounts for the tendency for everything in this poem to be seen in terms of the opposition of life and death" (Yenser 145). That is, Yenser understands the symbol in terms of constant change in the world: the presence of death in life. Similarly, James E. B. Breslin, viewing earth and lime as part of reality, suggests: "the first line of the third section's characterization of the poet's Great Aunt Sarah . . . implies her dissociation from the realities suggested by, say, earth and lime" (129). Following Yenser's interpretation of the symbol, I take it as the elemental composite of the world whose nature is incessantly moving and which, though contrasted, contains the harmony of the world.

nix/ from her bed of troublesome snacks and Tauchnitz classics," only when her sister, "needing a fourth for 'Auction,'" casts "a thirsty eye" to her. Indeed, Aunt Sarah's life is not far from the "naked Greek statues" at the Symphony Hall, "deathlike in the off-season summer," where she used to practice for the recital. The mood of death-in-life in Section Ⅲ undercuts the Winslows' overbearing world and also foreshadows Uncle Devereux's death in Section Ⅳ.

Although the fourth section centers on the death of Uncle Devereux, it begins with a sweet daydream:

> I picked with a clean finger nail at the blue anchor
> on my sailor blouse washed white as a spinnaker.
> What in the world was I wishing?
> . . . A sail-colored horse browsing in the bullrushes . . .
> A fluff of the west wind puffing
> my blouse, kiting me over our seven chimneys,
> troubling the waters. . . .
> As small as sapphires were the ponds: *Ouittacus, Snippituit, and Assawompset*, halved by "the Island."
> (*LS* 62, original italics and ellipsis)

So lovely a world seems to exult in its permanence, not aware of the grim reality of death. In particular, the pompously decorated pond of the Winslows stands in contrast to the impending death of Uncle Devereux. But in the following lines, the details of Uncle Devereux show that his world is full of things all of which are far from actual, normal life. For example, his rigid posture, "posed for 'the engagement photograph,'" and "severe/ war-uniform" connate his physical ossification; Mr. Punch, who "was tossing off a decanter of Scotch," appears to predict a bizarre object: "a water melon in hockey tights"; "La Belle France in a red, white and blue toga," who "was accepting the arm of her 'protector,'/ the ingenu and porcine Edward Ⅶ," looks quite unusual. The finest poster which contains the death of the young men "being bushwhacked on the veldt" directly anticipates the poster-ower's death in the following stanza.

From the first section to the beginning of the fourth section, Lowell has carefully established the context for the entrance of his uncle's death, not only by weaving together the decaying works of Grandfather, the aimless life of Grandmother and Aunt Sarah and the grotesque images in Uncle's posters, but also by connecting them with the universal cycle of seasonal change---Grandfather's summer house and then Uncle Devereux "closing camp for the winter." That is, it is not until the last section of the poem that Uncle Devereux's death and the young Lowell's knowledge of it appear. By delaying the entrance of the death, according to John Crick, Lowell illustrates that the uncle's death "offers no conclusion, no suggestion of fulfillment"; it just "takes its due place in an universal cycle."[4)]

The young Lowell's knowledge of death and decline latent in everything in the universe is shocking enough to frighten him:

---

4) John Crick, *Robert Lowell* (Edinburgh: Oliver & Boyd, 1974) 53.

My Uncle was dying at twenty-nine.
"You are behaving like children,"
said my Grandfather,
when my Uncle and Aunt left their three baby daughters,
and sailed for Europe on a last honeymoon . . .
I cowered in terror.
I wasn't child at all---
unseen and all-seeing, I was Agrippina
in the Golden House of Nero. . . . (*LS* 63)

The awareness of Uncle's dying at the peak of his life, his mental immaturity, and his untimely trip to Europe all combine to engender in the young Lowell a feeling of the absurdity of life. For Lowell as a boy, the most frightening fact concerning death seems that it can take place even at the prime time of our life. The five and a half year-old-boy is now Agrippina who knew the death plot against her by her treacherous son Nero; the boy, "unseen and all-seeing," is vaguely able to envision death in himself and others.

In the closing lines, most conspicuous is the young Lowell's staid description of the dying uncle:

Uncle Devereux stood behind me.
He was as brushed as Bayard, our riding horse.
His face was putty.
His blue coat and white trousers
grew sharper and straighter.
His coat was a blue jay's tail,
his trousers were solid cream from the top of the bottle.
He was animated, hierarchical,
like a ginger snap man in a clothes-press.

> He was dying of the incurable Hodgkin's disease. . . .
> My hands were warm, then cool, on the piles
> of earth and lime, a black pile and white pile. . . .
> Come winter,
> Uncle Devereux would blend to one color. (*LS* 64)

The repeated simple syntax reflects the young Lowell's sense of what his dying uncle feels: rigidity and bafflement. And like the contrast of cool black earth with warm lime, the lines quoted above hold apart a number of opposites. For instance, Uncle looks neat and dynamic like a riding horse, yet he is as pale as a dead person; Uncle's "blue coat and white trousers" grow stiff, but his coat is as free as a bird and his trousers; "solid cream" looks heavy; while "animated," Uncle is austere and "hierarchical." Here again, Lowell mixes warmth and coolness, and black and white, thereby establishing the co-existence of contrasting forces, the underlying structure of the world (the elemental entities of the harmony in the world). Based on such a recognition, Lowell comes to accept the fact that Uncle becomes closer and closer to death: "Come winter,/ Uncle Devereux would blend to the one color." At this point, all that Lowell as a boy has observed in his grandfather's farm has turned into the recognition of reality. In other words, the child's perceptions have accumulated and at last evolved into a recognition of the world.

On the literal level, this poem is about the poet-speaker's recollection of his childhood experience: his uncle's death. On the metaphorical level, the poet becomes aware of human mortality and the opposite forces which lend the world harmony. From such an awareness, the self may find a starting point to turn to maturity. In this sense, Hugh Staples points out that "My Last Afternoon" represents "an acceptance of the human condition."[5] And a new fashioning of the poet's self appears in the following poems of Part Four.

Discussing *Life Studies*, Katharine Willingford finds in Lowell "the splitting of the poet's ego into an experiencing half and an observing half."[6] Indeed, a number of poems in the volume include both perceptions; for instance, "91 Reverse Street" and almost all the poems in Part Ⅳ present a self which experiences as well as one which observes. Yet Willingford's view is too simple, for the poet's self is not the split ego which takes turns processing passive experience then active observation. The perceiving self of childhood turns into the evaluating, reflective self of the adulthood, and thus the two are linked.

In the poems which follow in Part Ⅳ, Lowell begins the process of connecting his early perceptions with his later evolutions and overcoming the alienation he might otherwise feel. He attempts to see his surroundings with new eyes. "Dunbarton," "Grandparents," and "Commander Lowell" are written with a changed vision. Self-fragmenta-

---

5) Hugh B. Staples 81. Marjorie G. Perloff endorses Hugh Staples: "the poet speaker, in the act of recalling his childhood, has learned that only by accepting the lives of others can one go beyond them" (152).

6) Katharine Wallingford, *Robert Lowell's Language of the Self* (Chapel Hill: U of North Carolina P, 1988) 91.

tion, the most prominent characterization in "91 Revere Street," is de-emphasized after "My Last Afternoon with Uncle Devereux," and Lowell's drifting and contradictory self begins to try to communicate with the world on its own terms.

Although the opening poem of Part Four, "My Last Afternoon," reaches a gesture of acceptance, this does not mean that Lowell has completely reconciled the warring forces around him. Lowell's critical view of his parents and grandfather still appears in several poems of the fourth part. In the poems following "My Last Afternoon," nevertheless, Lowell seldom directly condemns the cultural and religious values his grandparents could epitomize. This marks a considerable change from his previous attitude toward his grandparents that he expressed in *Lord Weary's Castle.*

In "Dunbarton," Grandfather Winslow is so affectionately depicted that he becomes a surrogate father during the time Lowell's father was still in the navy. Before, Lowell had accused his grandfather of leading a materialistic life in "In Memory of Arthur Winslow"; now, his affection for his grandfather is aroused. To express his love for him, for example, Lowell recalls touching moments: "he took the wheel himself---/ like an admiral at the helm./ Freed from Karl and chuckling over the gas he was saving,/ he let his motor roller-coaster/ out of control down each hill." Anger and derision, Lowell's usual response to his grandparents, are mostly replaced with lovely feeling:

My Grandfather found
his grandchild's fogbound solitudes
sweeter than human society.

When Uncle Devereux died,
Daddy was still on sea-duty in the Pacific;
it seemed spontaneous and proper
for Mr. MacDonald, the farmer,
Karl, the chauffeur, and even my Grandmother
to say, "your Father." They meant my Grandfather.

He was my Father. I was his son.
On our yearly autumn get-aways from Boston
to the family graveyard in Dunbarton,
he took the wheel himself---
like an admiral at the helm. (*LS* 65)

The young Lowell's isolation and his Grandfather's enjoyment of his grandson's solitude set up a new relationship between the two. And willingly accepting his Grandfather as father, Lowell not only insinuates his rebellion against his father, but also accentuates his grandfather's love for a grandson. For example, the way the grandfather drives is compared to "an admiral at the helm" which is a vicarious gratification for what his father lacks. Particularly the description of their annual visit to the family graveyard in Dunbarton heightens the intimacy between the two. As the poem progresses, this lovely relationship between grandfather and grandson is intensified once again in their combined tribute to their forebears:

Grandfather and I
raked leaves from our dead forebears,
defied the dank weather
with "dragon" bonfires. (*LS* 66)

This intimacy continues to develop to the extent that Lowell fabricates a memory in the fantasy of the closing lines, a new understanding of his family:

I saw myself as a young newt,
neurasthenic, scarlet
and wild in the wild coffee-colored water.
In the mornings I cuddled like a paramour
in my Grandfather's bed,
while he scouted about the chattering greenwood stove.
(*LS* 66-67)

In "Dunbarton," Lowell's new characterization of his grandfather does not hint at all of grandfather's aggressive behavior as contrasted with his spineless father. Instead, his affection for his grandfather dominates his recollection throughout the poem. His "yearly autumn get-aways from Boston" with his grandfather invests the poet with a lovely memory, and as Marjorie Perloff notes, the filial duty of tending the family graves which Lowell shares with his grandfather becomes "a rite of love."[7)]

"Grandparents" presents a similar emotion toward his Grandfather as in "Dunbarton," even though its narrator now is the adult Lowell. Recalling the now-dead grand-

7) Marjorie G. Perloff 35.

parents, Lowell endeavors to enclose them in sympathy. The vanished world of the grandparents is recovered, thus shedding a new light on the past and setting out an intimate relationship between the poet and his grandparents. Lowell, who inherited the family farm, maintains the same lifestyle as his grandfather: "I keep indoors, and spoil another season./ I hear the rattley little country gramophone/ racking its five foot horn: 'O Summer Time!'" Listening to music from grandfather's gramophone, he senses:

> *Ancien Régime* still keeps nature at a distance. Five
> green shaded light bulbs spider the billiards-table;
> no field is greener than its cloth,
> where Grandpa, dipping sugar for us both,
> once spilled his demitasse.
> His favorite ball, the number three,
> still hides the coffee stain. (*LS* 68)

What is remarkable here is Lowell's link between his own dull mood and a sudden uprising moment of love. By putting together the "*Ancien Régime*" world and the phrase "green shaded light bulbs spider the billiards-table" without pause, Lowell sparks an emotional moment from his past, recalling the usual hours which the poet spent with grandfather on the farm. Further, grandfather's billiard-ball, which is specifically highlighted as "the number three," galvanizes Lowell's present mood and thus makes the billiards-table cloth look greener than a farm's field; grandfather's affectionate gesture---"dipping sugar for both" arises again; besides, grandfather's favorite ball even "still hides the coffee stain," and that very ball creates a new image that brims with delight.

When he arrives at the instant of highest emotion, Lowell blends his moving memory with an irreverent reaction to his grandfather:

> Never again
> to walk there, chalk our cues,
> insist on shooting for us both.
> Grandpa! Have me, hold me, cherish me!
> Tears smut my fingers. There
> half my life-lease later,
> I hold an *Illustrated London News*---;
> disloyal still,
> I doodle handlebar
> mustaches on the last Russian Czar. (*LS* 69)

The adult poet becomes quite maudlin about the fact that grandfather is dead, never to return again. Nevertheless, the next line, "Tears smut my fingers," undercuts any sentimentality, for Lowell still can be "disloyal" to the world of "the last Russian Czar" symbolic of his grandfather.

"Grandparents" focuses mainly on the speaker's altered sentiment to his grandfather; even though still antagonistic toward the world which shaped his childhood, the poet-speaker reexperiences a touching moment in the past. More particularly, Lowell opens himself to the world and communicates with it. He shows that to have a dialogue with his past in detailed fashion is to understand himself and others; and further, it is to learn how to love others. By understanding himself and others, the poet continues to develop a self to the extent that he encompasses the past and thus recovers the lost reality in it. By conducting dialogue with the past, Lowell himself opens a possibility that fuses past and present, and his own self and others. Such a constructive attitude serves to restore his lost world in the poems following.

As *Life Studies* progresses, Lowell's world widens, and the poet moves on from conflict to reconciliation and from grievance to forgiveness. In this respect, "Commander Lowell" dramatically casts a new light on his listless father. While "91 Revere Street" focuses on the conflict over Father's resignation from the Navy as it emerged between his father and mother, "Commander Lowell" examines his father's failure in every civilian career he turned himself to; the former narrates the family conflicts from the child's point of view, but the latter reflects on Father's failures from a mature standpoint; the former has to do mainly with family matters, and the latter with complex matters like his father's lack of aptitude for a civilian career and his lack of worldly wisdom.

The first stanza, sketching his mother's closeness to her father in her personality, foreshadows Lowell's father's alienation from his wife:

> There were no undesirables or girls in my set,
> when I was a boy at Mattapoisett---
> only Mother, still her Father's daughter.
> Her voice was still electric
> with a hysterical, unmarried panic,

when she read to me from the Napoleon book. (*LS* 70)

In the succeeding lines, Lowell, by exhibiting his rebellious behavior toward his mother ("... I, bristling and manic,/ skulked in the attic,/ and got two hundred French generals by name"), concedes Father's victimization by Mother as well as expressing compassion toward Father. Thus, Mother's world, briefly summed up in a few opening lines, reveals that it is Mother herself who accelerates Father's failures and humiliation in his civilian career.

In "91 Revere Street," Lowell sees his father as pathetic: "Father resigned from the service in 1927, but he never had civilian career; he instead had merely twenty-two years of the civilian life" (LS 15). But in "Commander Lowell," the adult Lowell describes his father in a more sympathetic eye, though addressing the same defeated father. For example, Lowell tries to see his father's defeated civilian career as understandable in some sense:

> "Bob," they said, "golf's a game you really ought to
> know how to play,
> if you play at all."
> They wrote him off as "naval,"
> naturally supposed his sport was sailing.
> Poor Father, his training was engineering!
> Cheerful and cowed
> among the seadogs at the Sunday yacht club,
> he was never one of the crowd. (*LS* 71)

Since his father is not interested in the common life style

of high society, he only becomes ridiculed, never accustomed to Boston high society. It is implied that his father's subsequent defeats in his civilian career are quite natural. By stressing his father's background and former career, Lowell makes the "seadogs at the Sunday yacht club" superficial, thus defending his father. Insinuating that dilettantism in high society assures the defeat of Lowell's father's civilian career, Lowell reveals his compassion for his father. Unlike "91 Revere Street," this narration of his father's defeat in his civilian career underlines Lowell's sympathy toward his father.

The defense of his father culminates at the end of the fourth stanza. His pathetic retirement from the navy, though done against his will, is just the beginning of his humiliation; first of all, Lowell's father "deeded Mother his property," the signal of a total submission to his wife. After repeated dismissals, all that remains for Lowell's father to do is to debase himself into being the client of his own business. Needless to say, Father's relationship with Mother worsens. We now find that Lowell's father has lost all links with reality, thus falling into fantasy: "Night after night,/ *à la clarté déserte de sa lampe*,/ he slid his ivory Annapolis slide rule/ across a pad of graphs---." The French quotation from Charles Baudelaire's "Le Voyage" serves to illuminate "the tone of his father's lamplit excursions to nowhere."[8] Finally, Lowell's father

8) In *Imitations*, Lowell translates the line of Baudelaire ("*Ah! que le monde est grande à la clarté des lampes!*") into "how grand the world in the blaze of the lamps." For further detail, see Mark Rudman, *Robert Lowell* (New York: Columbia UP, 1983) 68.

"squandered sixty thousand dollars" in speculations; bankrupt both in mental and material terms, his father is reduced to the nadir of his life. Lowell concludes this poem with an attempt to redeem his father from his failures. The following episodes are not potent enough to praise his father as a successful career man, but Lowell seeks to shed a new light on his father through them:

> Smiling on all,
> Father was once successful enough to be lost
> in the mob of ruling-class Bostonians.
> As early as 1928,
> he owned a house converted to oil,
> and redecorated by the architect
> of St. Mark's School. . . . Its main effect
> was a drawing room, "longitudinal as Versailles,"
> its ceiling, roughened with oatmeal, was blue as the sea.
> And once
> nineteen, the youngest ensign in his class,
> he was "the old man" of a gunboat on the Yangtze. (*LS* 72)

By recounting his father's youth, Lowell attempts to regenerate "Commander Lowell's reputation"[9] and restore to his father even the slim dignity which Commander Lowell might have possessed. Most important, reviewing his father's life in different terms, Lowell seems to liberate himself from the mother's world described in "91 Revere Street." He thus expands his own world.

"Terminal Days at Beverly Farms" presents Lowell's father's last year, a year spent in great pain. With compas-

9) Karl Malkoff 110.

sion, Lowell focuses on his father who behaves courageously. Father has moved to Beverly Farms, close to the Boston doctors but having "no sea-view," suggesting a complete end to his lifetime vision. He underwent "two coronaries," afflictions which must have greatly weakened his physical strength. Besides, he is so isolated that his best friend is now only the "little black *Chevie*,/ garaged like a sacrificial steer/ with gilded hooves." But his heart is still in the navy, and Lowell's father even bribes the local dealer "to quickly deliver a car without chrome." The car helps to revive memories of the naval career that preceded his humiliations in civilian life:

> Each morning at eight-thirty,
> inattentive and beaming,
> loaded with his "cal" and "trig" books,
> his clipper ship statistics,
> and his ivory slide rule,
> Father stole off with the *Chevie*
> to loaf in the Maritime Museum at Salem.
> He called the curator
> "the commander of the Swiss Navy." (*LS* 74)

All that Lowell's father does may look ridiculous, but in order to highlight his father's strength, Lowell accentuates even his father's smallest efforts to complete his dream. To Lowell's maturing self, his father, who drives his car to the Maritime Museum and names the curator the commander, appears to make himself a real Commander of the navy. To the adult Lowell, Commander Lowell is no longer the symbol of defeat and humiliation. Thus, the concluding lines, describing his physically healthy father ("His vision was still twenty-twenty"), present a man stoical in the face of death: "After a morning of anxious, repetitive smiling,/ his last words to Mother were:/ 'I feel awful.'"

Beginning with its "unbecoming femininity,"[10] "Father's Bedroom" displays the romantic dream Lowell's father had in his youth. The poet-speaker, examining the remains in his father's bedroom, discovers a copy of Lafcadio Hearn's *Glimpses of Unfamiliar Japan*, whose "warped olive cover/ was punished like a rhinoceros hide." This book, given to the young Robbie by Lowell's grandmother, motivated Lowell's father to become a navy commander:

> "this book has had hard usage
> on the Yangtze River, China.
> It was left under an open
> porthole in a storm." (*LS* 75)

The book is a metonym for Commander Lowell's life. Though its cover has been "punished like a rhinocerous hide," its "hard usage" does not mean hard reading on the ship, but neglected treatment by its owner. On the one hand, such a treatment of the book exhibits his father's unfulfilled dream which was initially inspired by the book's exotic subject, and partially reflects his father's lack of initiative to make his dream come true. On the other hand, the scribbled words, boldly confessing his

10) Stephen Yenser 152.

treatment of the book, show the Commander's commitment as a naval officer during his participation in the Chinese civil war. That is, this poem begins with a description of the feminine features of father's bedroom, but it underlines father's strength by recalling his father's small yet admirable deed as a navy commander.

"For Sale" is the poem which displays Lowell's maturing self in terms of his altered attitude toward his mother. Although he continues to regard his father, his father's house and furniture merely serve to create an empty, dry, and lifeless atmosphere after the owner's death; that is, Lowell's focus shifts from his father to mother and his mother's response to her husband's death. In the adult Lowell's eye, Commander Lowell's death at least had a great impact on his wife:

> Ready, afraid
> of living alone till eighty,
> Mother mooned in a window,
> as if she had stayed on a train
> one step past her destination. (*LS* 76)

As we have seen in "91 Revere Street" and "Commander Lowell," Lowell's parents spent their loveless marital life in constant conflict. In the light of their previous relationship, her feeling here about her husband is surprising. Lowell now finds a relationship between Father and Mother which was not as unfavorable as described in previous poems. Lowell highlights the "interdependence" between his parents,[11] and the partitioned worlds between a passive father and an active mother, between weakness and strength, are mingled together into an indivisible one.[12] The adult Lowell's reading of the lovely relationship between father and mother also embodies his own affection for his parents. Undeniably, this view by Lowell stems from the mature self; it expresses a fusion of the opposite after a continued dialogue between the poet's self and his surroundings. That is, Lowell's gradual re-recognition of his family draws him toward a shared relationship between the world and himself.

In "Sailing Home from Rapallo," Lowell escorts his mother's body from Italy to her family graveyard in Dunbarton. As shown in "For Sale," Lowell, speaking of his mother, mourns her death though he mingles his compassion with a slight criticism of her ambitious quest. (He expresses a similar sentiment toward the dead maternal relatives who pursued the same kind of dream as his mother, blending compassion with light condemnation toward her relatives buried in Dunbarton). Mother's body departs from Italy in the midst of "the whole shoreline of the *Golfo di Genova*" "breaking into fiery flower" which looks like a wreath dedicated to her body. Yet Mother's "*Risorgimento* black and gold casket," resembling Napoleon's, is carried in the first-class, which reminds us of Mother's pursuit of luxury and beauty in "91 Revere Street." This treatment even after death, whether done or not by her

---

11) Karl Malkoff 112.

12) Karl Malkoff observes the disappearance of a dichotomous division between the passive father and the active mother in the closing lines of the poem (112).

demand, partially accounts for what she was. Now matured, however, the adult poet is less critical of the way in which many of the Winslows lived their lives.

As the filial duty sketched in "Dunbarton" shows, Lowell has altered his previous attitude toward the Winslows, his mother's family. In the following lines, Lowell exhibits his compassion for his mother and her family:

> While the passengers were tanning
> on the Mediterranean in deck-chairs,
> our family cemetery in Dunbarton
> lay under the White Mountains
> in the sub-zero weather.
> The graveyard's soil was changing to stone---
> so many of its deaths had been midwinter.
> Dour and dark against the blinding snowdrifts,
> its black brook and fir trunks were as smooth as masts.
> A fence of iron spear-hafts
> black-bordered its mostly Colonial grave-slates. (*LS* 77)

Though beautifully depicted, the family cemetery where Mother's body will be buried, exhibits cold, dark and lonely images, and thus enhances Lowell's compassion for his mother: "Dour and dark against the blinding snowdrifts,/ its black brook and fir trunks were as smooth as masts."

The description of his father's tomb in Dunbarton illustrates that Lowell's conflict with his maternal relatives still lingers, even if much mitigated. For example, Lowell's father is drawn as the "only 'unhistoric' soul," and he is inappropriate in the cemetery just like his Latin motto which "seemed too businesslike and pushing." Thus, Lowell's father appears to be not only dominated by his wife's family ethic (here summed up as dominated by coldness), but also lonely in the midst of "twenty or thirty Winslows and Starks." Understated, Lowell's sentiment toward his maternal relatives once again expresses sympathy toward his father and indirectly underlines the theme of victimization which prefigures his mother's victimization in "During Fever."

Lowell ends with a depiction of his mother's body in compassionate terms. In death, mother looks almost as pathetic as his father:

> In the grandiloquent lettering on Mother's coffin,
> *Lowell* had been misspelled *LOVEL*.
> The corpse
> was wrapped like *panettone* in Italian tinfoil. (*LS* 78)

What Lowell's mother sought to capture throughout her life is reflected in the misspelled yet grandiloquent-lettered coffin. Seen in the light of her enthusiastic chase of "Beauty" and "Luxury," she here becomes quite abject and trivial. In the next lines, Lowell's mother's corpse, "wrapped like *panettone* in Italian tinfoil," makes itself more pathetic. As Marjorie Perloff observes, the "weighty substances" like stone, iron, marble, and diamond "yield to the everyday household product"---tinfoil, and this transformation also serve to create "the triviality, ordinariness, and pathos of Mrs. Lowell's death."13)

Most important, Lowell's mother is still different from her husband. Nevertheless, his mother comes closer to his father in terms of her descent to ordinariness. Such an identification of mother and father in death suggests the poet-speaker's attempt to create a reconciliation between his parents as well as with himself. The interdependence between his parents Lowell presents in "For Sale" is developed into an identification in a narrow sense by the maturing Lowell.

Lowell opens "During Fever" by referring to his young daughter who seems to succeed to the austere family ethic of the Winslows: "my daughter in fever/ flounders in her chicken-colored sleeping bag./ 'Sorry,' she mumbles like her dim-bulb father, 'sorry.'" By drawing on characteristics found in his young daughter, Lowell continues trying to understand his mother, thereby breeding his forgiveness of his mother. He illustrates his grandfather's legacy in his mother, a legacy which victimized his parents and himself. Lowell once lived in the very world as shaped by his mother as the successor of her father:

> Often with unadultered joy,
> Mother, we bent by the fire
> rehashing Father's character---
> when he thought we were asleep,
> he'd tiptoe down the stairs
> and chain the door. (*LS* 79)

---

13) Marjorie G. Perloff 10.

The world Lowell and his mother shared is so narrow as to exclude his father. Intimacy with mother thus enhances father's alienation. More significant, rather than the conspiratorial world of mother and son, the poet seems to stress his father's tolerance toward the exclusive relationship between his wife and son. By doing so, Lowell underlines his father's difference from his maternal grandfather whose strictness toward his daughter made her a victim of his ethic.

The next stanza sketches the psychological state of the victimized mother. As in "91 Revere Street," the poet examines her obsessive pursuit of beauty and her coldness, a manifestation of psychological trouble. Recollecting the decoration of his mother's "master-bedroom," Lowell once again uncovers her obsession of the perfect combination of beauty and luxury, which merely turns out pointless. Her artificial decorations--- "Italian china fruity/ with bunches and berries/ and proper *putti*" represent her cold, breakable world. An "electric blanket" and "hot water bottle," both answer any need she might have for warmth. The picture of Mother's bedroom sums up a miserably strained life.

The last stanza presents how strict Lowell's grandfather was to his daughter:

> Mother, you smile
> as if you saw your Father
> inches away yet hidden,
> as when he groused behind a screen
> over a National Geographic Magazine,

whenever young men came to court you
back in those settled years of World War One.
Terrible that old life of decency
without unseemly intimacy
or quarrels, when the unemancipated woman
still had her Freudian papá and maids! (*LS* 80)

As we have already seen, Charlotte Winslow's marriage to Commander Lowell was not made as an independent decision by her. It was due in part to Arthur's admiration for the Lowells' social fame that their marriage took place. Lowell's mother spent her whole life under her father's influence and relied on him as a Napoleon or a Siegfried even after her marriage. The poet here again presents his mother as being closely attached to her father. Lowell's mother is defined and dominated by her father who used to stay "inches away yet hidden." Thus, "Freudian papá" is the father-figure who dominated, repressed her, and prevented her from fashioning her own world. The father-figure ingrained in Mother has hindered her marital life and even her "nuptial bed." Lowell now approaches the realization that his mother may also be a victim. Such a recognition leads Lowell to forgive his mother and have compassion toward her. Alan Williamson also points out that since Lowell has found what he shares with his parents, he becomes able to forgive his father's weakness and his mother's coldness.[14)]

Indeed, the first section of Part Ⅳ has shown how the poet arrives at a point where he can forgive the fam-

---

14) Alan Williamson 73.

ily members with whom he had been at war. Through his poetic dialogue, the adult Lowell has dissolved his enmity with parents and relatives. As his self moves on, however it contains a number of contradictions. Toward his relatives, for instance, the poet still harbors antagonistic sentiments; he still seeks the seed of his parents' unhappiness in his grandfather, even though stressing the lovely intimacy between his grandfather and himself ("Dunbarton" and "Grandparents"). While Lowell expresses bitter feeling toward his mother in "Commander Lowell" (who, he thinks, accelerated his father's downhill in civilian career), he becomes sympathetic toward his mother in "Sailing Home from Rapallo," "For Sale" and "During Fever."

Despite the scattered contradictions, however, there is no doubt that Lowell's world has expanded to the extent that it embraces others and commingles them with itself. Lowell's world will continue to widen in the poems that follow as he works through communication with others. Although the adult Lowell still has conflicts with his family members, he has now admitted the possibility that he is able to accept them and even embrace them in communication and in love.

Chapter 5

Madness, Tranquilization, and the Self

Maurice Merleau-Ponty claims:

> . . . each present permanently underpins a point of time which calls for recognition from all the others, so that the object is seen at all times as it is seen from all directions and by the same means, namely the structure imposed by a horizon. The present still holds on to the immediate past without positing it as an object, and since the immediate past similarly holds its immediate predecessor, past time is wholly collected up and grasped in the present.[1]

1) Maurice Merleau-Ponty, *Phenomenology of Perception* 69.

Elaborating on the interrelationship between the past and the present, he implies that the past, through an incessant interaction with the present, turns into meaning; that the future also breeds its meaning in relation with the immediate past. In the first section of Part IV in *Life Studies* (from "My Last Afternoon" to "During Fever"), Robert Lowell, engaging himself with his family members with whom he was in conflict, seeks to locate his identity, with a belief that his self cannot be understood apart from his family which constitutes his past. Placing himself in relation to his family leads to a new recognition of his present self and a fashioning of a new relationship with his family members. More specifically, Lowell's communication with his past helps him perceive the world and himself, and the past bears on the meaning in the present. Although Lowell does not completely reconcile himself with his family members, he grows sympathetic toward them and accepts them into the new world that is his poetry.

The first section of Part IV is a new portrait of his family and of himself which Lowell sketches from the standpoint of the present. But as Part IV proceeds to its end, Lowell shifts focus to himself. The poet-speaker himself becomes the central theme of his poems, and ultimately his own madness and imprisonment are explored in relation to others in a world viewed as maddening. The second section of the fourth part is an examination of the suffering poet's present in a hostile world. As Ian Hamilton observes, it is "Part Four that actually bears the name '*Life Studies.*'"[2)] Actually, the poet-speaker proceeds to expand his own self in its interaction with the world.

From the opening poem of *Life Studies*, Lowell has gradually established a context in which to define himself in the world. While Part I outlines Lowell's view of civilization in a historical perspective, Part III, in specific terms, examines the condition with which, Lowell believes, modern writers are confronted. Lowell's vision of the contemporary world is expressed in his sketch of writers whose predicament condenses the madness of the world. The tormenting circumstance in Part III prefigures the similar situation Lowell is in in the second section of the fourth part. In the second section of Part IV, Lowell combines the previously described context of the modern world set forward in Part III and his maturing self, and thereby comes to investigate himself. The estrangement and isolation of the four writers in Part III anticipate Lowell's own situation in the second section of Part IV. Before discussing the poet's self in the second section of the fourth part, thus, it is necessary to examine the condition of the modern world and the lives of the four writers in it as characterized in Part III.

"Ford Madox Ford" presents an artist's predicament that stems from a cultural atmosphere adverse to the value of art:

> you emerged in your "worn uniform,
> gilt dragons on the revers of the tunic,"
> a Jonah---O divorced, divorced
> from the whale-fat of post-war London! Boomed,

---

2) Ian Hamilton 261.

cut, plucked and booted! In Provence, New York . . .
marrying, blowing . . . nearly dying
at Boulder, when the altitude
pressed the world on your heart

(*LS* 49, original ellipsis)

Like the Hebrew Prophet Jonah, who was swallowed by a whale and forgotten, Ford was "divorced" from post-war London and also neglected by the America public during his lecture tour. Needless to say, the estrangement of the writer is a reflection of the cultural values of a society more prone to commerce than art. As Richard Fein notes, the frustration the British novelist underwent comes close to that of the modern writers in Ezra Pound's "Hugh Selwyn Mauberly,"[3] where Pound examines the fate of the artist in the cultural decadence of a commercialized age.

As Lowell shows, due to public indifference, Ford remained almost completely segregated from an appreciation by his culture. Lowell compares the writer's suffocating condition to a fish out of water:

and your audience, almost football-size,
shrank to a dozen, while you stood
mumbling, with fish-blue-eyes,
and mouth pushed out
fish-fashion, as if you gagged for air. . . .

(*LS* 50, original ellipsis)

3) Richard J. Fein, *Robert Lowell* (Boston: Twayne, 1979) 68.

In the following lines, the novelist's divorce from so maddening a culture is expressed through repulsive animals like the toad and the elephant; besides this, the frequent use of words such as "gassed voiceless," "mumbling," "mammoth mumbler," and "huffing" underscores a communication gap between the writer and the audience in a decaying culture. Lowell, using these forceful contrasts, underlines Ford's brilliant achievement as the artist who wrote "Soldier,/ the best French novel in the language." That is, despite Ford's genius, he was neglected because of the audience's lack of understanding, and thus he ended as a failure both as artist and individual. The theme of imprisonment by an external force which begins in "A Mad Negro Soldier Confined at Munich" appears here again and foreshadows Lowell's own institutionalization in "Waking in the Blue" and "Memories of West Street and Lepke."

In "For George Santayana," Lowell addresses a philosopher and man of letters who suffered alienation from his time due to his own religious and aesthetic beliefs. George Santayana, born in Spain but educated in America, moved from America to England to Paris and finally to Rome where he lived until his death in a convent. As his constant exile exhibits, he was a liberal in his attitude toward religion and culture. For instance, Santayana, though proud of his Latin cultural background, was not solely inclined to Spanish culture; he was personally fond of Catholicism but not a believer; although he cared nothing for its religious belief, he, as an aesthete, loved the form of Catholicism. In this poem, Lowell pays special attention to Santayana's unaltered loyalty to Catholicism.

Different from other writers, Santayana's alienation results from his own ambiguous standpoint to Catholicism. Santayana himself chooses to keep himself apart from the world as a "free-thinking Catholic infidel":

> There at the monastery hospital,
> you wished those geese-girl sisters wouldn't bother
> their heads and yours by praying for your soul.
> "There is no God and Mary is His Mother." (*LS* 51)

Even though he was dying in a monastery hospital, the writer refused to depend on a religious benediction and kept his usual distance from Catholicism: ""There is no God and Mary is His Mother.""

In the second stanza, Lowell draws on Santayana's transcendence of his isolation and on his subtle combination of religion and atheism. To the poet, George Santayana looks triumphant, even if he was buried "outside the consecrated ground." A determined atheist, Santayana died "still unbelieving, unconfessed and unreceived,/ true to your boyish shyness of the Bride." Above all, Lowell stresses that he was pure and true as a child, although an unbeliever. Thus Santayana is described in paradoxical terms as contradictory to Christianity:

> Old trooper, I see your child's red crayon pass,
> bleeding deletions on the galleys you hold
> under your throbbing magnifying glass,
> that worn arena, where the whirling sand

and broken-hearted lions lick your hand
refined by bile as yellow as a lump of gold. (*LS* 52)

Santayana, depicted as a Christian gladiator, is not antagonized by his adversaries who show a friendly gesture by "lick[ing] your hand/ refined by bile as yellow as a lump of gold." As one "refined by bile," the philosopher looks more pure. On the first level, Lowell admires Santayana's ability to resolve the conflict between Catholicism and atheism. On the second level, the poet emphasizes that Santayana reconciled his self and the world. In this respect, Santayana wins admiration from Lowell, and Santayana, as a rebellious atheist, forecasts Lowell the conscious objector. His reconciliations further anticipate the poet-speaker's reconciliation with an outer, hostile world in "Skunk Hour."

While the two previous poems commemorate the older writers as "father-figures,"[4] the following two poems of Part III, "To Delmore Schwartz" and "Words for Hart Crane," are addressed to his fellow poets, presenting Lowell's own version of the outer world. That is, the former sketches a modern cultural condition under which writers are doomed to madness, as well as Lowell's own *Angst* in the world, while the latter bitterly satirizes cultural corruption.

"To Delmore Schwartz," through its eccentric actions and images, shows Lowell's vision of the world and draws a self-portrait of the poet.[5] Choosing a drugged

---

4) J. D. McClatchy, *White Paper: On Contemporary American Poetry* (New York: Columbia UP, 1989) 105.

poet as a model and a drunk animal as a talisman, Lowell illustrates the condition of the world where he writes poetry. For the poet-speaker and his fellow poet, the outer world appears to be threatening, and they hope to find a way to cope with that threat. For instance, their grotesque behavior and the decoration of their room with a "stuffed duck" seems to be their best effort to relieve themselves of "universal *Angst*":

> Your stuffed duck craned toward Harvard from my trunk:
> its bill was a black whistle, and its blow
> was high and thinner than a baby's thumb;
> its webs were tough as toenails on its bough.
> It was your first kill; you rushed it home,
> pickled in a tin wastebasket of rum---
> it looked through us, as if it'd died dead drunk.
> You must have propped its eyelids with a nail,
> and yet it lived with us and met our stare,
> Rabelaisian, lubricious, drugged. And there,
> perched on my trunk and typing-table,
> it cooled our universal
> Angst a moment, Delmore. We drank and eyed
> the chicken-hearted shadows of the world.
>
> (*LS* 53, original italics)

5) In a letter to William Meredith, Lowell writes about Delmore Schwartz that: "I think the later poems have more flow and joy than suited his genius. His destiny seemed the most hopeful of any young poet in 1940, then the downward roads, some germ in the mind, *the most dismal story of our generation perhaps, and maybe a lot more to the writing than one knew*" (quoted in Ian Hamilton 350, italics mine). The italicized passage seems to reflect what Lowell thinks he shares with his contemporary poets in "To Delmore Schwartz."

Since they consider the world insane, Lowell and Schwartz take on madness as a role, a defense against the maddening world's incursion. In other words, against the madness they perceive in the world, they endeavor to protect themselves by way of their invented madness. Lowell underscores that unlike the nineteenth-century poet, Coleridge, who chose to retreat toward madness, modern poets must accept the madness and frustration of their time: "*We poets in our youth begin in sadness:/ thereof in the end come despondency and madness*" (*LS* 54, original italics). They fabricated madness, but hope to make it contribute to their life and art.

The last poem of Part III, "Words for Hart Crane," presents a poet who was neglected by the public like Ford Madox Ford but who stubbornly persisted in his rebellious stance toward his society. What is most conspicuous in the poem is the candor with which Lowell condemns a decaying culture. Denying the standard of the Pulitzers, for example, Crane attacks the corruption of the prize, one of the most prestigious literary awards in America, and despises those who won the Pulitzers as "dupe[s]/ or screw[s] who flushed our dry mouths out with soap." Since he is too candid and defiant, it is Crane himself who courts his own alienation:

> "Because I knew my Whitman like a book,
> stranger in America, tell my country: I,
> *Catullus redivivus*, once the rage
> of the Village and Paris, used to play my role
> of homosexual, wolfing the stray lambs

> who hungered by the Place de la Concorde.
> My profit was a pocket with a hole.
> Who asks for me, the Shelley of my age,
> must lay his heart out for my bed and board." (*LS* 55)

Self-declared outcast, Crane incisively rejects American culture which is materialistic: "[I] scattered Uncle Sam's/ phoney gold-plated laurels to the birds." All that his disobedience to society's standard brings him is poverty: "my profit was a pocket with a hole." Even though the poem is spoken by Hart Crane, undeniably, its message is Lowell's view of a corrupted society whose value system is topsy-turvy. This poem also prefigures the poet-speaker imprisoned when he boldly protested against the government.

As we have examined it, Part III portrays cultural disruption as manifested in modern writers. The four poems mirror the poet-speaker's vision of the modern world as well as offering a brief portrait of the young Lowell. As Lowell recognizes the elements of decay in the culture, so he expresses his spiritual fellowship with the four writers; furthermore, he admires those writers who boldly struggled with various predicaments in the world. Most important of all, the third part of *Life Studies* constitutes the background for the world's condition under which he will be located in the fourth part's second section.

Although Lowell has a pessimistic world vision, he does not seek to withdraw from that hostile world; rather, he chooses to plunge into it and investigate himself in the midst of its darkness and hostility, by divulging his suffering psyche unreservedly. Particularly in the second section of the fourth part, the poet-speaker unmitigatedly recounts his past experiences and encourages them as reality rather than concealing or embellishing them. Unlike his previous poems, therefore, here Lowell does not condemn the world which he recognizes is filled with fragmentation. Instead, by engaging the world, he seeks to locate his self and establish his identity in the world.

As *Life Studies* progresses, we find the poet-speaker moving on to maturity in terms of the way he recognizes the world. He repeatedly tells us that he is now forty. Although he has not completely reconciled with the external forces which restrain him, he seldom harbors as much hostility toward his family members and others as he once did. Lowell understands the people who are in the world. Seeing himself as one of them and feeling sympathetic toward them, he willingly shares their torments. Generally speaking, Lowell, in the fourth part's second section, identifies himself with the world's tormented people. In "Waking in the Blue" and "Memories of West Street and Lepke," for example, while Lowell wants to separate himself from his institutionalized inmates, he nontheless accepts their presence in the world.

As I have pointed out earlier, the poet-speaker's self has gradually aggrandized itself, and he treated his past as it concerned his family with a sympathetic eye. In the second section of the fourth part, the poet-speaker ruminates from a mature perspective on his tortuous past and on his fellow inmates, both in McLean's, a mental institution, and West Street Jail. Lowell's self has now developed to an extent that it embraces not only his family but also a world in which others appear. That is to say, just as Lowell views the outer world as alienating to its inhabitants (like Ford Madox Ford, George Santayana, Delmore Schwartz, and Hart Crane), thus acquiring an expression of sympathy for them, so he would understand his inmates as alienated and in need of sympathy in the same way. Most important, in this same second section, Lowell arrives at a self-discovery: Lowell recognizes in himself "a nonentity" which he found in his father.[6] Such a recognition of himself leads the poet to cast a warm and compassionate eye on his fellow inmates. It is at this point of *Life Studies* that Lowell's world appears conspicuously broadened. In this respect, Mark Rudman is right when he finds "an extended family" in Lowell's institution poems: "[a]fter the family portraits in the early parts of the 'Life Studies' section, Lowell's imagination explodes and he writes four major poems: 'Waking in the Blue,' 'Memories of West Street and Lepke,' 'Man and Wife,' and 'Skunk Hour.' From this point on it is as if his nuclear family had dissolved; he begins to *treat the world as an extended family*"[7] (italics mine). By having investigated his painful experiences so far, Lowell comes to an awareness that he is also one of the tranquilized in the maddening world. Especially in the second section of Part IV, the poet-speaker portrays himself in his own world as one who is as confined as others': in the mental hospital

---

6) James E. B. Breslin 137.

7) Mark Rudman, *Robert Lowell: An Introduction to the Poetry* (New York: Columbia UP, 1983) 71.

in "Waking in the Blue"; in the jail in "Memories of West Street and Lepke"; in the prison of marriage in "Man and Wife" and "'To Speak of Woe That Is in Marriage.'"

In "Waking in the Blue," the adult Lowell centers on madness as a primary subject of his poetry for the first time in *Life Studies.* The poet-speaker presents through his sanatorium experience his own sense of confinement and his helpless passivity before a large social insitution. Because the poet-speaker's situation is fearful, this poem begins with a yearning toward detachment ("What use is my sense of humor?"), yet ends with affinity and sympathy for the inmates ("We are all old-timers,/ each of us holds a locked razor").

"Waking in the Blue" opens with the "night attendant, a B. U. sophomore," the only normal character in this poem. Although the night guard feels physically tired, he is able to read *The Meaning of Meaning*, a philosophical work, thanks to his mental sanity. Thus, the guard is in sharp contrast with the poet who is wide awake and tense. The poet-speaker confesses such a tension in himself:

> Azure day
> makes my agonized blue window bleaker.
> Crows maunder on the petrified fairway.
> Absence! My heart grows tense
> as though a harpoon were sparring for the kill.
> (This is the house for the "mentally ill.") (*LS* 81)

The "Azure day" here seems to reflect the inner topography of the poet in the mental hospital. Whether it is bright or not, the daybreak must be felt as deep-blue to the poet-speaker, a feeling which continues to darken gradually until the end of the first stanza. Mentally insecure, the poet-speaker senses that his death is imminent: "as though a harpoon were sparring for the kill." The inner and outer landscapes in the first stanza sum up the poet's present, the state of being completely helpless in this institution. Such a precarious feeling extends to the poet's awareness of his own helpless confinement: "(This is the house for the 'mentally ill')."

In the following lines, the poet's two inmates, "ossified young," are miserably reduced to animals, an attribute that all in this poem share. Former Harvard all-American fullback, Stanley, seems no more than a sea animal, even though he still maintains the physical vigor of his glorious days: "still hoarding the build of a boy in his twenties/ as he soaks, a ramrod/ with the muscle of a seal." Besides this, since the one-time football star confines himself to his narrow world, he never talks with his fellow inmates, and this lack of communication seems to imply the deterioration of his mentality:

> A kingly granite profile in a crimson golf-cap,
> worn all day, all night,
> he thinks only of his figure,
> of slimming on sherbet and ginger ale---
> more cut off from words than a seal. (*LS* 81)

Lowell understands why the football star is remote from reality; he cannot overcome the narcissism of his early achievement. Even when petrified with his former glory and enclosed in a sanatorium, Stanley still tries to preserve the past: "A kingly granite profile in a crimson golf-cap,/ worn all day, all night." Ironically, such an effort, degrading his former glory more, only doubles his misery as well as increases his animality. The portrait of this helpless inmate prepares for the poet's own situation which is similar to Stanley's.

Lowell presents another fellow inmate who was also once a brilliant Harvard man: a member of "Porcellian '29," an elite Harvard club. Though "a replica of Louis XVI," Bobbie looks like an animal: "redolent and roly-poly as sperm whale," just like Stanley. Nevertheless, his behavior shows he still lingers over his past: "he swashbuckles about in his birthday suit/ and horses at chairs." But such a ridiculous behavior reinforces only his abnormality.

Indeed, these two figures, whose mentality halted at the heyday of their life, are prefigured in the death of Lowell's Uncle Devereux at his prime. Physically still maintaining animal-like strength yet mentally hardened in their twenties, the two Harvard graduates have lost track with reality, due to "partly the result of an intense early narcissism, tied to achievements."[8] Since they devoted

8) Alan Williamson 75. On the almost same ground, Rabbit Angstrom, the protagonist of John Updike's *Rabbit Run*, can be considered to be a person who becomes "ossified young" due to the glory he enjoyed as a highschool basketball star early in his life. Rabbit, confining him-

their youth to meeting the standard their culture established, they became victims of that culture. That is, they are subjugated by a huge external force---culture. Here lies Lowell's sympathy with defeated people as well as his criticism of American capitalism which incites competition.

"[O]ssified young," the "victorious figures of bravado" are under a double imprisonment: not only are they confined to a mental hospital, but they have enclosed themselves in their own narrow world established when young. Thus, no channel of communication exists with others, and only empty hours encompass all the inmates:

> In between the limits of day,
> hours and hours go by under the crew haircuts
> and slightly too little nonsensical bachelor twinkle
> of the Roman Catholic attendants.
> (There are no Mayflower
> screwballs in the Catholic Church.) (*LS* 82)

Although the figures are only physically restricted to the sanatorium, time itself, according to Marjorie Perloff, is also in itself a confinement. Just as the glory gained in their youth failed to go beyond Harvard, so time has not progressed at all since their school days. Even now the hours cannot reach beyond the hospital and just pass by "under the crew haircuts." As a result, their lives become nothing but "a meaningless vacuum."[9] At this point of

---

self to his old fame, fails to adapt himself to ordinary social life, and as his name suggests, he is reduced to an animal with addiction to sex.

9) Marjorie G. Perloff 168.

the poet's observation of his inmates, his claustrophobic feeling arrives at its culmination.

Lowell, examining others, comes to know his own imprisonment in a suffocating world, and thus his anxiety grows. But at the same time, he realizes that he is similar to them in many aspects. The poet-speaker's investigation of his old fellow inmates in the long run leads to his identification with them. By juxtaposing "the Roman Catholic attendants" and "Mayflower screwballs," Lowell reveals that he also undeniably belongs to "these shipwrecks of Yankee culture."[10] The poet finally recognizes himself, imprisoned with others in the world:

> After a hearty New England breakfast,
> I weigh two hundred pounds
> this morning. Cock of the walk,
> I strut in my turtle-necked French sailor's jersey
> before the metal shaving mirrors,
> and see the shaky future grow familiar
> in the pinched, indigenous faces
> of these thoroughbred mental cases,
> twice my age and half my weight.
> We are all old-timers,
> each of us holds a locked razor. (*LS* 82)

Lowell has so far investigated the products of Boston culture, a culture ingrained in the poet himself. His "hearty New England breakfast" and proud walk in his "turtle-necked French sailor's jersey" are closely associated

10) Mark Rudman 74.

with the behavior the two Harvard men, representing the ruined Yankee culture, still carry. Especially, Lowell's choice of the word "strut" underlines the arrogant aspect of Boston's cultural credo stored in him. At last, the poet recognizes himself as one of "these thoroughbred mental cases." When he says, "We are all old-timers," he emphasizes the helpless confinement they all share. Because his fellow inmates have neither a sober present nor a secure future, they are defined only in terms of their remote past. Similarly, Lowell, having observed himself mirrored in his fellow inmates, finds his future "pinched" and small. For the inmates, including Lowell himself, all that remains now is the wasted hours, helplessly falling into passivity: "each of us hold a locked razor." The "mental shaving mirrors" and "a locked razor" reinforce their firm imprisonment as well as the affinity among the inmates which Lowell accentuates through the animal attributes which everybody in this poem shares: the B. U. sophomore "catwalks"; Stanley is twice compared to "a seal"; Bobbie is like "a sperm whale"; Lowell is "Cock of the walk."

Lowell's identification with his inmates results from a self-discovery that like his fellow inmates, he is also defined and victimized by a culture which harbors madness in it. Surprisingly, in the face of this disturbing awareness of himself, the poet-speaker openly accommodates himself to self-knowledge. Such a submission subsequently leads to the understanding of others. In a similar vein, Karl Malkoff suggests that the conclusion of "Waking in the Blue" carries "reverberations": ". . . just as his father's world has become enmeshed with his own, so his world becomes part of his father's. The 'old-timer' reminds us of Commander Lowell and makes us aware of the locked razor that passive, overwhelmed man had for so many years carried within him."[11] Needless to say, the "reverberations," a result of the poet's communication with his past, indicates a further widening of the poet's world.

In "Home After Three Months Away," Lowell examines himself after he returned home from his shock treatment in McLean's. Considering how to recover the time wasted in the mental hospital, the poet interrogates his present and future. The three-month-confinement brought several signs of passage of time. For example, the "seven horizontal tulips" have almost withered and "the baby's nurse" has left the house now. The only thing that, Lowell finds, remains the same is his daughter Harriet who still expresses unaltered affection for him:

> Dimpled with exaltation,
> my daughter holds her levee in the tub.
> Our noses rub,
> each of us pats a stringy lock of hair---
> they tell me nothing's gone.
> Though I am forty-one,
> not forty now, the time I put away
> was child's-play. After thirteen weeks
> my child still dabs her cheeks
> to start me shaving. When

---

11) Karl Malkoff 113.

we dress her in her sky-blue corduroy,
she changes to a boy,
and floats my shaving brush
and washcloth in the flush. . . .
Dearest, I cannot loiter here
in lather like a polar bear. (*LS* 83)

The daughter's exaltation is a great consolation to the anxious poet-speaker. Seen in light of his daughter's stable intimacy with him as well as of her clean bath, the "kingly reference"[12]---"my daughter holds her levee in the tub"---totally differentiates his return home from Mclean's which, by contrast, is associated with Stanley in his long, dirty tub as well as Bobbie, "a replica of Louis XVI" yet "redolent and roly-poly as a sperm whale." In fact, the time he spends with his daughter helps him "put away" as "child's-play" the time wasted in the hospital. His daughter also reminds him that he can shave freely without metal shaving mirrors and locked razors, the symbols that firmly held the hospital inmates together. Despite the consolation he finds at home, however, the poet recognizes that the mental hospital still heavily lin-

---

12) Ian Hamilton reads all the "kingly references" in "Waking in the Blue" as the same reference as in "Home After Three Months Away": "The kingly references---'Is Richard now himself again,' 'my daughter holds her levee in the tub'---force us back to Stanley in his 'long tub' and Bobbie, the 'replica of Louis XVI,' Lowell's McLean's playmates" (Hamilton 255). But it seems to me that "the kingly reference" in "Home After Three Months Away" is totally different from the ones in "Waking in the Blue" and "Memories of West Street and Lepke" in that it is a kind of expression of affection for his daughter, particularly of her unchanged love to him.

gers in him: "Dearest, I cannot loiter here/ in lather like a polar bear." In other words, his sense of partial security, gained from his release from the hospital and the sight of his daughter, is undercut by his anguished memory of McLean's.

Such a mixed feeling makes the poet-speaker look deep into what and where he is now:

> Recuperating, I neither spin nor toil.
> Three stories down below,
> a choreman tends our coffin's length of soil,
> and seven horizontal tulips blow.
> Just twelve months ago,
> these flowers were pedigreed
> imported Dutchmen; now no one need
> distinguish them from weed.
> Bushed by the late spring snow,
> they cannot meet
> another year's snowballing enervation. (*LS* 84)

The garden, far from the garden of Eden, seems to accommodate the poet-speaker's worried present. He is quite fearful about that very fact: is he completely cured or not? The images mirror the poet's precarious vision of his future. For example, there appears the "coffin's length of soil" cared for by a "choreman"; the tulips planted a year ago, though once "pedigreed/ imported Dutchmen" (like "Mayflower screwballs"), have now changed into weeds; besides, they are now "Bushed" so that they are unable to endure "another year's snowballing enervation." Accordingly, the poet reaffirms that though back home from the mental hospital, he is still in a highly restless condition: "I keep no rank nor station./ Cured, I am frizzled, stale and small."

On the literal level, "Home After Three Months Away" is a lament for the time wasted in McLean's. Yet on the metaphorical level, it is a self-portrait of the poet-speaker's anxious present. In other words, the poet's self-possessed examination of himself leads into an unmitigated portrait of his present; he is still mentally unstable, in spite of his physical release from the hospital. The withered flowers, emblematic of the poet himself, also show that he is similar to his fellow inmates who faced downfalls early in their lives. Although painful, this examination of the sanatorium experience lends Lowell a recognition of himself and an identification with his former inmates. Here again a dialogue with his past brings the poet to a self-discovery that also serves to enlarge his world as well as to help him understand others.

"Memories of West Street and Lepke" presents us with the poet-speaker as a social being. As long as he is in the world, Lowell shows, his surroundings become an undeniable locus of his identity. In other words, whether he wants or not, the poet constantly interacts with his society, a dialogue from which the meaning of his self is fashioned. When he says, "Ought I to regret my seedtime?," the poet is asking himself if he can now reject all that he did in the past. Rather than detaching himself from his surroundings, this question underlines the close relationship between his self and his society.

The poem begins with a description of the tranquillized circumstance of the 1950s, replete with the apolitical offsprings of the period. The poet-speaker himself is part of that social milieu:

> Only teaching on Tuesdays, book-worming
> in pajamas fresh from the washer each morning,
> I hog a whole house on Boston's
> "hardly passionate Marlborough Street,"
> where even the man
> scavenging filth in the back alley trash cans,
> has two children, a beach wagon, a helpmate,
> and is a "young Republican." (*LS* 85)

The poet appears to spend restful days, merely "teaching on Tuesdays" and reading the rest of the weekdays; the pajamas the poet wears all the time illustrate the distance between himself and his community; that is, he rarely makes contact with people around him. The word "hog" emphasizes the poet's physical leisure, in line with the overall atmosphere of the community---"hardly passionate Marborough Street." Humorously, Lowell sketches the materialistic affluence of a society: a person who, though "scavenging filth in the back alley trash cans," enjoys seeming happiness; the scavenger is comically depicted as a "'young Republican.'" Most important, the poet's description of the character's way of life merely discloses the spiritual emptiness amid external abundance, the dominant mood of the period. Alan Williamson speaks of the 1950s as "a period of timidity in the personal life as well: of earlier marriages and more stable careers; more artists in the academy, and fewer eminent bohemians; of an 'adjustment'-oriented psychiatry, and a popularized existentialism, in which the critique of absolute values appeared without the concomitant emphasis on engaged, contingent choice, and so rationalized an accepted hedonism. Ecstasy and a self-created life style were considered dubious goals for the individual."[13] Under such a mood, Lowell considers his present.

Lowell looks back on his days in the West Street Jail where he was imprisoned for his political statements during World War II. The poet distinguishes himself from other prisoners in the jail, suggesting a sense of superiority to his fellow inmates. As the "sooty clothesline entanglements" implies, the poet stresses a dubious borderline of conscience and crime, by pointing out the same treatment accorded the conscientious objector as the criminal. For example, his wartime protest against the government ("telling off the state and president") left him alongside a criminal, Negro boy "with curlicues/ of marijuana in his hair." Abramowitz, "the fly-weight pacifist," the only person in the jail who could talk about metaphysics with him, was beaten by the "Hairy, muscular, suburban" Hollywood pimps.

In the final stanza, the adult Lowell recalls the well-known gangster who is the most brutal among the prisoners but now severely tamed. Paradoxically, the adult poet finds a similarity with himself and this murderer:

13) Alan Williamson 77.

. . . *Murder Incorporated's* Czar Lepke,
there piling towels on a rack,
or dawdling off to his little segregated cell full
of things forbidden the common man:
a portable radio, a dresser, two toy American
flags tied together with a ribbon of Easter palm.
Flabby, bald, lobotomized,
he drifted in a sheepish calm,
where no agonizing reappraisal
jarred his concentration on the electric chair---
hanging like an oasis in his air
of lost connections. . . .

(*LS* 86, original italics and ellipsis)

The leader of a murder syndicate, though lobotomized and condemned to death, enjoys privileged life, surrounded by "the things forbidden the common man." In a sense, the Czar is close to the scavenger in terms of material possessions and moral emptiness. Superficially, however, the murderer looks far different from the young Lowell, except for the fact that they shared the same jail. Lowell was not only a conscientious objector who claimed pacifism against the government, but also an intellectual who "yammered metaphysics" with another radical pacifist, Abramowitz. Yet when the poet's memory expands to include Czar Lepke, he comes to the realization that he resembles the murderer. The peculiarity in Lepke that Lowell finds horrifying is located in the adult Lowell himself. Like Lepke, for instance, he now enjoys a privileged life "only teaching on Tuesdays"; like Lepke, who is tamed and normalized, he had an electric shock treatment from McLean's and is now back home "frizzled, stale and small." At this point of the poem, all differences with the inmates, particularly with Lepke, are dissolved, and his present identity becomes almost identified with that of a murderer.

Because the inmates are characterized as quite distinct among themselves, especially from the young Lowell, it seems that what they do share is that they are helpless prisoners altogether. As the poem proceeds, however, what Lowell has found in all the prisoners turns out to be all the possibilities in himself. Interestingly, all the inmates are linked to Lowell, due to their distinctiveness. Like Abramowitz, Lowell was a pacifist and challenged the government and the president, but he failed to make his dream come true; he, though a conscientious objector, is similar to the Hollywood pimps in that he was quite wild when he expressed himself against the government; like the marijuana-smoking boy, his mind is not clear because of the shock treatment in a mental hospital.

As I have pointed out, a theme of fragmentation penetrates *Life Studies*. This theme is mirrored by the mad people and "the tranquilized man" and forms the dominant image of *Life Studies*.[14] For example, the Negro soldier, Delmore Schwartz, Bobbie and Stanley fell into madness and lived in fantasy; the Negro soldier, Lepke and Lowell himself were all tranquilized.

Part IV closes with two poems about a marriage which seems to clash tranquilization with madness.

---

14) Karl Malkoff 114.

Throughout *Life Studies*, marriage is considered as a form of incarceration just like Lowell's imprisonment in McLean's and the West Street Jail, partly because of the impression the poet-speaker received from his parents' unhappy marital life. In "Man and Wife" and "'To Speak of Woe That Is in Marriage,'" the poet presents marriage as an extension of "a locked razor" in a different sense. In "Man and Wife," the young Lowell contrasts himself to his father who, innately lackadaisical, pathetically submitted himself to his wife and finally "deeded Mother his property." As described in "91 Revere Street," the young Lowell was rebellious against his parents. The adult Lowell, wild and prone to violence, challenged even the government. Whereas his father fell into fantasy and lost touch with reality, Lowell must examine his present by engaging his past experience. The opening line of "Man and Wife," "Tamed by *Miltown*, we lie on Mother's bed," reminds us of that very bedroom where Lowell's parents frequently clashed. Yet unlike his parents, Lowell and his wife seem to be at peace. As the poem proceeds, however, Lowell's dependence on his wife and her dominance are underlined. Their relationship comes to resemble that of his parents. Indeed, Lowell is depicted as a child, a point which reveals his passivity to his wife: "All night I've held your hand,/ as if you had/ a fourth time faced the kingdom of the mad---its hackneyed speech, its homicidal eye---/ and dragged me home alive." Just like his mother in "91 Revere Street," Lowell's wife is characterized by her conspicuous rhetoric. At this point in the poem, their relationship looks quite similar to that of his parents: he describes himself as "too boiled and shy/ and poker-faced to make a pass,/ while the shrill verve/ of [his wife's] invective scorched the traditional South."

At last, his wife turns into a Charlotte Winslow, Lowell's mother, and the poet-speaker perceives himself taking over his father's place:

> Now twelve years later, you turn your back.
> Sleepless, you hold
> your pillow to your hollows like a child;
> your old-fashioned tirade---
> loving, rapid, merciless---
> breaks like the Atlantic Ocean on my head. (*LS* 87)

Just as Lowell observes a similarity between himself and Lepke the murderer in "Memories of West Street and Lepke," so he recognizes his father in his own present. Although his father withdrew himself toward fantasy and the young Lowell, a wild pacifist, became a violent protester, father and son converge here in a shared identity. The world into which Lowell looks is horrifying: "your old-fashioned tirade---/ loving, rapid, merciless---/ breaks like the Atlantic Ocean on my head." Yet it is a world Lowell actively recalls, and he accepts it as the world where he now lives.

"'To Speak of Woe That Is in Marriage'" draws on the agony in marriage. But in a metaphorical sense, this poem, similar to "A Mad Negro Soldier," is a microcosm of the world Lowell has described so far. Reversing his own mother and father, in his marriage it is the wife who is submissive and the husband who is wild. The husband is drunk and unfaithful, but the wife is sober and faithful. She speaks:

> "The hot night makes us keep our bedroom windows open.
> Our magnolia blossoms. Life begins to happen.
> My hopped up husband drops his home disputes,
> and hits the streets to cruise for prostitutes,
> free-lancing out along the razors' edge.
> This screwball might kill his wife, then take the pledge.
> Oh the monotonous meanness of his lust. . .
> It's the injustice . . . he is so unjust---
> whiskey-blind, swaggering home at five." (*LS* 88)

Like the relationship between the mad Negro soldier and his girlfriend, this marriage tends toward violence, and the husband's passion resembles the mad Negro's in "A Mad Negro Soldier." But even as this marriage looks chaotic, it is still maintained. And it is the energetic sex that ties the husband to his wife: "'Gored by the climacteric of his want,/ he stalls above me like an elephant.'" Interestingly enough, this marriage verges on madness yet contains its own vitality, in contrast to that of his father and mother in "Man and Wife." And this theme of vitality foreshadows the pure and vital moment in "Skunk Hour."

Although this poem mainly addresses a personal madness, it is not difficult to see that such madness is closely associated with the failure of various external forces, and with moral, spiritual, social, and cultural collapses. Indeed, this poem, as Karl Malkoff points out, weaves all sorts of disintegration as "part of the texture of Lowell's psyche."[15)]

The poet-speaker has viewed himself in a number of contexts in the world and found his own incarceration and alienation reflected in it. Such an awareness brings the poet to identifying with the people in the world.

The second section of the Part IV consists of Lowell's most unreserved confession of his past experience. By revealing and questioning himself in the present, Lowell comes to understand the madness of the outer world and finds himself within it. Lowell's observation of others leads to his present identity. Especially in the second section of the fourth part, the poet's careful positioning himself in the world helps him understand others as well as sympathize with them. Thus, the more Lowell understands his self in the world, the more he grows compassionate toward others. Lowell's world now transcends his family and he has forged a shared identity within the world. Indeed, it is a point of clear maturity, in which all the world's inhabitants are viewed by him as suffering within the world. Yet Lowell seems to suggest that they can be redeemed from their suffering by their sympathy for each other as well as by their communication with the world.

---

15) Karl Malkoff 116.

Chapter 6

"Skunk Hour": Completing *Life Studies*

Some critics have pointed out that Robert Lowell's *Life Studies* has a perfect structure as a collection of poems. Interestingly enough, the poems in *Life Studies,* written in different periods, are well arranged to form a narrative chain. *Life Studies* opens with the poet "On the train from Rome to Paris," which implies Lowell's metaphorical journey to locate himself in the world." Such a journey of exploration in his life traverses various external forces like civilization, family, culture and society, all of which are finally woven into the suffering poet of "Skunk Hour." *Life Studies*, as it approaches its close, gradually narrows its focus to the poet-speaker himself. Lowell's broad account of civilization in his opening poem converges in his final poem on a brief moment of personal anguish. But that anguish, while personal, is situated distinctly in the world.

Before we read "Skunk Hour," let us summarize each part of *Life Studies* briefly. Part I, a setting for the whole book, announces the theme of a disintegrating civilization which will continue in different forms throughout *Life Studies*. Part II, an autobiographical prose memoir, brings forward the family division in Lowell's father and mother, and the psychological breakdown of the young Lowell himself. Drawing on four modern writers such as Ford Madox Ford, George Santayana, Delmore Schwartz, and Hart Crane,[1)] Part III foreshadows the poet's own madness and imprisonment. In the first section of Part IV, Lowell brings up again the disintegration in his family yet at the same time seeks to fashion a reconciliation between his family members and himself. The second section of Part IV, which opens with a poem about institutionalization, focuses on the poet's private agony as it reacts to the external forces in the world.

---

1) Steven Gould Axelrod observes a spiritual communion between Lowell and the four writers: "They [four poems] establish Lowell's sense of spiritual kinship to brilliant and tormented writers---Ford Madox Ford, George Santayana, Delmore Schwartz, and Hart Crane---all of whom in some way contributed to his growth as a poet, and all of whom endured an exile from society prefiguring his own. These poems, comprising a kind of parabolic autobiography, then yield to the explicit autobiography of the 'Life Studies' themselves, which directly exposes Lowell's own particular set of circumstances, his own flawed being." See Steven Gould Axelrod, *Robert Lowell: Life and Art* (New Jersey: Princeton UP, 1978) 106-107.

All the poems in *Life Studies* are interwoven with one another. As a group, they become a context for the poet's own life study[2]. As the structure of the book merges with the growth of one person, the poet draws closer to self-awareness. That is, Lowell, in recalling his experiences, comes to recognize himself and others in the world. The poet's understanding of the world accompanies an understanding of himself which enlarges his inner world. In that way, the world and the poet's self inter-relate to each other in *Life Studies.*

"Skunk Hour" unfolds like all of *Life Studies* in that it first presents the poet's perception of the world and then shows the recognition of himself in the world. Likewise, it epitomizes the modern world and the suffering poet in it. Presenting a picture of the modern world in its first four stanzas, "Skunk Hour" can be broken down into three parts: the sketch of an overall crisis in the modern world, followed by the poet-speaker's presentation of his psychological state, and ending with the discovery of a momentary sense of vitalization.

---

2) John Crick discusses the structure of *Life Studies* in a similar terms: "The poems tend to overlap; themes and motifs are announced, discarded, and then taken up later. To mention only one example, there is the motif of grandparents; in 'Beyond the Alps', we have a picture of self-confident Victorian grandparents; then we come nearer home, with several picture of Lowell's grandparents, and the refuge and consolation they represented for the young Lowell in retreat from his immediate parents---so much of Life Studies is about surrogate parents. Near the end of the book, lowell reflects that he has a daughter 'young enough to be my granddaughter.' Simple objects also recur and take on the force of symbols: for example, cars, beds and razors." John Crick, *Robert Lowell* (Edinburgh: Oliver & Boyd, 1974) 49.

In the first four stanzas, Lowell offers characters who show the various physical and mental insecurities as they are embedded in the modern world:

> Nautilus Island's hermit
> heiress still lives through winter in her Spartan cottage;
> her sheep still graze above the sea.
> Her son's a bishop. Her farmer
> is first selectman in our village;
> she's in her dotage.
>
> Thirsting for
> the hierarchic privacy
> of Queen Victoria's century,
> she buys up all
> the eyesores facing her shore,
> and lets them fall.
>
> The season's ill---
> we've lost our summer millionaire,
> who seemed to leap from an L. L. Bean
> catalogue. His nine-knot yawl
> was auctioned off to lobstermen.
> A red fox stain covers Blue Hill.
>
> And now our fairy
> decorator brightens his shop for fall;
> his fishnet's filled with orange cork,
> orange, his cobbler's bench and awl;
> there is no money in his work,
> he'd rather marry. (*LS* 89)

This community characterizes an overall atmosphere under which the poet-speaker lives, and central themes in *Life Studies.* For example, the "hermit heiress" has lost her sanity; her son has become a bishop who does not bear offspring; her farmer becomes a chief administrative authority in the island, a fact that suggests political topsy-turviness. Most important, all these facts combine to indicate that the family is in dissolution. The mother is so selfish that she is not interested in familial commitment at all; rather, a fanatic consumer, she purchases "all/ the eyesores facing her shore, and lets them fall" for nothing. All that she does is eccentric as well as self-indulgent; also, she is both anti-religious and anti-social.

The degeneration of the island includes the decay of its social structure in cultural, ethical, moral and economic terms. "The season's ill" and "a red fox stain covers Blue Hill" characterize a general condition of the community. For example, the "summer millionaire," whose only "nine-knot yaw" is sold to "lobsterman" after his death, seems to be false and hollow. The falsity in the summer millionaire leads us to the corruption of a false lover in the next stanza. The decorator, whose work ethic has been degraded, uses the fisherman's corks and cobbler's bench and awl for the adornment of the tourist shop rather than for fruitful labor[3]; without a heart for marriage, this homosexual decorator sees marriage only as another ploy to save his withering business. Needless to say, the loveless, sterile marriage shows us another part of the distorted social culture of the island.

---

3) John Frederick Nims 91.

Throughout the first part, all that Lowell suggests is fragmentation manifested in the inhabitants. The world consists of a self-indulgent old lady who grows abnormal, a dead short-term millionaire and a fraudulent decorator. Such figures suggest mental instability, declining affluence, self-centeredness, lovelessness and a loss of social order. And in some sense, these inhabitants parallel aspects of the Lowell family (his mother, his father, grandparents and his wife) as well as the lives of his inmates in McLean's and the West Street Jail, all of whom Lowell painfully describes throughout *Life Studies.*

The sweeping state of culture in the first part comes close to the modern world Lowell has examined throughout *Life Studies.* And the disintegration he points up in this miniaturized modern world finds a counterpart in Lowell's past experience and his mental illness. That is, this poem moves from a picture of the external world to a landscape of the poet's inner world:

> One dark night,
> my Tudor Ford climbed the hill's skull;
> I watched for love-cars. Light turned down,
> they lay together, hull to hull,
> where the graveyard shelves on the town. . . .
> My mind's not right.
>
> A car radio bleats,
> "Love, O careless Love. . . ." I hear
> my ill-spirit sob in each blood cell,
> as if my hand were at its throat. . . .
>
> (*LS* 90, original ellipsis)

In the fifth stanza, written in the past tense, Lowell reveals his personal experiences. Just as social illness dominates the island, so darkness rules the poet's world. "The season's ill," a symptom of decaying community, turns to "My mind's not right"; the loneliness of the demented heiress and the lovelessness of decorator are epitomized in the poet-speaker's own experiences. Lowell is in an abysmal world without light where love is reduced to mechanical sex. This breakdown in outer world shifts to the personal breakdown in the poet. As both observer and participant, Lowell sees the hell in his inner world, and his spiritual deprivation arrives at this culmination: "I myself am hell;/ nobody's here---." Commenting on his own poem, Lowell named the night "An Existentialist night," and he recalled "a passage from Satre or Camus about reaching some point of final darkness where the one free act is suicide."[4] If it is an existentialist night, Lowell's creation of hell in himself exhibits "the qualities of a hero."[5] Undeniably, it is the poet's courage that keeps him from retreating from the personal crisis to some transcendental reality. He remains instead on the earth. He will "self-surrender" to the world.[6]

Strangely enough, it is a family of skunks which provide Lowell with a life-giving air:

4) John Frederick Nims 107.

5) Steven Gould Axelrod 129.

6) John Frederick Nims 93.

nobody's here---

only skunks, that search
in the moonlight for a bite to eat.
They march on their soles up Main Street:
white stripes, moonstruck eyes' red fire
under the chalk-dry and spar spire
of the Trinitarian Church.

I stand on top
of our back steps and breathe the rich air---
a mother skunk with her column of kittens swills the garbage pail.
She jabs her wedge-head in a cup
of sour cream, drops her ostrich tail,
and will not scare. (*LS* 90)

An ugly, repulsive animal, skunks nonetheless display vitality by engaging themselves in the search for "a bite to eat." The skunks "moonstruck eyes' red fire" imply passion and activity in contrasts to "the chalk-dry and spar spire/ of the Trinitarian Church" which recalls the decay of the spiritual world. In particular, the mother skunk's commitment to her kittens shows her family in a composure which preserves love, a point that Lowell's family had lacked; the mother skunk is fertile ("kittens") and active as well as sound and sane. All the traits Lowell finds in the skunks stand in distinct contrast to the many characters in *Life Studies* who are lonely, insane, incarcerated and tranquilized. Moreover, Lowell seems to imply that the skunk's healthiness and freedom differ from his own spiritual instability and construction under the pressure of various external forces.

The healthiness of the skunks lends the poet vitality, offering a possibility for survival. Thus "Skunk Hour" is Lowell's hour, because in it Lowell encounters a vitalizing moment after a long struggle with forces both in and outside him. The skunk family represents what Lowell has long sought out. He finds in the integrity of the skunk family a sense of his own identity.

The moment of "the rich air" in "Skunk Hour" results from a courageous quest for the self in the world, a quest that entails confronting painful experience. As he declared he would in "Beyond the Alps," the poet has explored himself within the outer world by re-experiencing the torment external forces imposed on him. But even when most anguished, Lowell declines any recourse to move toward a transcendental reality at all. Rather, Lowell accepts the world in its torment, and locates himself in it. Thus what Lowell draws forward in the closing lines of "Skunk Hour" embodies the co-existence of the self within the world, the result of the poet's constant engagement with the world and others. Through an ongoing dialogue with others in the world, Lowell has enlarged his inner world to include others. As he does in Part IV, in "Skunk Hour" the poet-speaker has extended himself to an extent that he can revitalize his fractured sense of identity, even in the world of the repulsive, even at the zenith of his agony. This is not a retreat but a firm recognition of his presence in the world.

The triumph of "Skunk Hour" is the triumph of *Life*

Studies. Lowell's language has now built a "house of being" in the world. But it is not the world of "absolute freedom" Sartre promotes in *Being and Nothingness*; in Maurice Merleau-Ponty's words, it is the world which is neither "objective" nor "subjective," but "intersubjective," because Lowell has constructed his own world by engaging himself in the world.[7] It is a world in which, as Merleau-Ponty says, quoting St.-Exupéry, that "man is but a network of relation, and these alone matter to him."[8]

---

7) Maurice Merleau-Ponty, *Signs* 92-97.

8) Maurice Merleau-Ponty, *Phenomenology of Perception* 456.

Bibliography

Axelrod, Steven Gould. *Robert Lowell: Life and Art.* New Jersey: Princeton UP, 1978.

Bell, Daniel. *The End of Ideology: On the Exhaustion of Political Ideas in the Fifties.* New York: The Free Press, 1960.

Bly, Robert. *American Poetry: Wilderness and Domesticity.* New York: Harper & Row Publishers, 1990.

Breslin, Paul. *The Psycho-Political Muse.* Chicago: U of Chicago P, 1987.

Breslin, James E. B. *From Modern to Contemporary American Poetry, 1945-1965.* Chicago: U of Chicago P, 1987.

Brown, J. A. C. *Freud and the Post-Freudians.* London: Penguin Books, 1972.

Cook, Albert. *Prisms: Studies in Modern Literature.* Bloomington: Indiana UP, 1967.

Cooper, Philip. *The Autobiographical Myth of Robert Lowell.* Chapel Hill: U of North Carolina P, 1970.

Crick, John. *Robert Lowell.* Edinburgh: Oliver & Boyd, 1974.

Detweiler, Robert. *Story, Sign, and Self: Phenomenology and Structuralism as Literary-Critical Methods.* Philadelphia: Fortress, 1978.

Ehrenpreis, Irvin. "The Age of Lowell." *Robert Lowell: A Collections of Critical Essays.* Ed. Thomas Parkinson. Englewood Cliffs, N. J.: Prentice-Hall, 1968. 75-97.

Eliot, T. S. *The Sacred Wood.* London: Methuen, 1964.

Fein, Richard J. *Robert Lowell.* 2nd ed. Boston: Twayne Publishers, 1979.

Freud, Sigmund. *The Ego and the Id.* London: Hogarth Press, 1950.

______________. *Civilization and Its Discontents.* Trans. James Strachey, New York: Norton, 1961.

Fromm, Erich. *Man for Himself: An Inquiry into the Psychology of Ethics.* New York: Rinehart & Co., 1947.

Hall, Donald. *Contemporary American Poetry.* Baltimore: Penguin Books, 1965.

Hamilton, Ian. *Robert Lowell: A Biography.* New York: Random House, 1982.

Hassan, Ihab. *Contemporary American Literaturre 1945-1972: An Introduction.* New York: Frederick Ungar Publishing Co, 1973.

Heidegger, Martin. *Being and Time.* Trans. John Macquarrie and Edward Robinson. New York: Harper & Row Publishers, 1962.

Horney, Karen. *The Neurotic Personality of Our Time.* New York: Norton, 1937.

Lacan, Jacques. *Écrits: A Selection,* Trans. Alan Sheridan. New York: Norton, 1977.

Laing, R. D. *The Politics of Experience.* New York: Ballantine Books, 1967.

Leibowitz, Herbert. "Robert Lowell: Ancestral Voices." *Salmagunda* 1 (1966): 25-43.

Lipset, Seymour M. "A Changing American Character?." *Culture and Social Character.* Eds. Seymour M. Lipset and Leo Lowenthal. New York: The Free Press of Glencoe, 1961.

Lowell, Robert. *Life Studies and For the Union Dead.* New

York: Farrar, Straus and Giroux, 1964.

____________. *Lord Weary's Castle and The Mills of the Kavanaughs.* New York: Harcourt Brace Jovanovich Publishers, 1946.

____________. *Poems: 1938-1949.* London: Faber & Faber. 1960.

____________. "On 'Skunk Hour.'" *The Contemporary Poet as Artist and Critic.* Ed. Anthony Ostroff. Boston: Little, Brown & Company, 1964. 107-110.

Malkoff, Karl. *Escape from the Self.* New York: Columbia UP, 1977.

Mannheim, Karl. *Ideology and Utopia.* Trans. Louis Wirth and Edward Shils. New York: Harcourt Bruce Jovanovich, 1936.

Marcuse, Herbert. *One-Dimensional Man.* Boston: Beacon Press, 1964.

______________. *Eros and Civilization: A Philosophical Inquiry into Freud.* Boston: Beacon Press, 1966.

Martin, Jay. "Grief and Nothingness: Loss and Mourning in Lowell's Poetry." *Robert Lowell: Essays on the Poetry.* Eds. Steven Gould Axelrod and Helen Deese. New York: Cambridge UP, 1986.

Mazzaro, Jerome. *The Poetic Themes of Robert Lowell.* Ann Arbor: U of Michigan P, 1965.

McClatchy, J. D. *White Paper: On Contemporary American Poetry.* New York: Columbia UP, 1989.

Merleau-Ponty, Maurice. *Phenomenology of Perception.* Trans. Colin Smith. London: Routlege & Kegan Paul, 1962.

____________________. *The Primacy of Perception.* Trans.

William Cobb Evanston, IL: Northwestern UP, 1964.

____________________. *Signs*. Trans. Richard C. McCleary. Evanston, IL: Northwestern UP, 1964.

____________________. "What Is Phenomenology?" Trans. John F. Banner. *Cross Current* 6 (1956): 59-71.

Miller, Jr., James E. *The American Quest for a Supreme Fiction: Whitman's Legacy in the Personal Epic*. Chicago: U of Chicago P, 1979.

Mills Jr., Ralph J. *Cry of the Humans: Essays on Contemporary American Poetry*. Urbana: U of Illinois P, 1975.

Mills, C. Wright. *The Power Elite*. New York: Oxford UP, 1956.

_______________. *White Collar: The American Middle Classes*. New York: Oxford UP, 1951.

Pearce, Roy Harvey. *The Continuity of American Poetry*. Princeton: Princeton UP, 1961.

Perloff, Marjorie. *The Poetic Art of Robert Lowell*. Ithaca: Cornell UP, 1983.

Pound, Ezra. *Selected Prose 1909-1965*. Ed. William Cookson. New York: New Directions, 1973.

Riesman, David and others. *The Lonely Crowd: A Study of the American Character*. New Haven: Yale UP, 1950.

Rosenthal, M. L. *The New Poets: American and British Poetry since World War II*. New York: Oxford UP, 1967.

Rudman, Mark. Robert *Lowell: An Introduction to the Poetry*. New York: Columbia UP, 1983.

Saussure, Ferdinand de. *Courses in General Linguistic*, Trans. Roy Harris. London: Duckworth, 1983.

Seidel, Frederick. "Interview with Robert Lowell." *Robert*

Lowell: A Portrait of the Artist in His Time. Ed. Robert Boyers. New York: David Lewis, 1964.

Sontag, Susan. *Illness as Metaphor.* New York: Farrar, Straus and Giroux, 1978.

Spiegelberg, Herbert. *The phenomenological Movement: A Historical Introduction.* The Hague: Martinus Nijhoff Publishers, 1984.

Spiller, Robert. *The Cycle of American Literature: An Essay in Historical Criticism.* New York: Farrar, Straus and Cudahy, 1962.

Staples, Hugh B. *Robert Lowell: The First Twenty Years.* New York: Farrar, Straus and Cudahy, 1962.

Sullivan, Harry Stack. *The Fusion of Psychiatry and Social Science.* New York: W. W. Norton & Co., 1964.

Wallingford, Katharine. *Robert Lowell's Language of the Self.* Chapel Hill: U of North Carolina P, 1988.

Weber, Max. *The Protestant Ethics and the Spirit of Capitalism.* Trans. Talcott Parsons. New York: Scribners, 1930.

Williamson, Alan. *Pity the Monsters: The Political Vision of Robert Lowell.* Westport, Connecticut: Greenwood Press, 1986.

Witek, Terri. "Robert Lowell's Token's of the Self." *American Literature* 63 (1991): 712-26.

Yenser, Stephen. *Circle to Circle: The Poetry of Robert Lowell.* Berkeley: U of California P, 1975.